Codependent—
NOW
WHAT?

IT'S NOT YOU—
IT'S YOUR
Programming

LISA A. ROMANO

outskirtspress
DENVER, COLORADO

Outskirts Press, Inc.
http://www.outskirtspress.com

ISBN: 978-1-4787-7203-3

Outskirts Press and the "OP" logo are trademarks belonging to Outskirts Press, Inc.

PRINTED IN THE UNITED STATES OF AMERICA

TABLE OF CONTENTS

DEDICATION

This book is dedicated to the grandmother I never knew who committed suicide when my father was four years old. Grandma Pauline was married to a violent alcoholic. Back in the 1940s there were few options for a young wife who was married to an addict. Her suicide is an event that I have always perceived as a cry for help at a time in history that had yet to understand the paralyzing nature of fearing what it might mean to appear *imperfect*.

INTRODUCTION

I was a young married mother of three small children when my life began spinning violently out of control. Asthma, amongst other inflammatory diseases, had gained ground in my knotted body. "Lisa, you better listen to your body, because your body is listening to you," my doctor said during an emergency visit to his office one bright and sunny midweek afternoon. "There is no physical reason for you to be this sick right now," he continued, evidently as pissed off as he was concerned.

I remember sitting up and leaning forward on the exam table like asthmatics do when they are consciously trying to draw air into the constricted highways and byways that make up the human lungs during severe asthma attacks. Exhausted due to poor blood oxygen levels, it was a struggle to keep my eyes open as my doctor rushed around the exam room and ordered his nurse to start me on intravenous steroids. Too tired to be embarrassed by the saliva that was being spat into the oxygen mask, it was all I could do not to close my eyes and fall into a deep sleep while sitting up and being poked.

In spite of being deathly ill that afternoon, my ears were still working. As if the words my doctor spoke were branded onto my brain, I could not get them out of my head. Through the dazed web of confusion that had become my mind, something deep within I had not yet become comfortably acquainted with began to stir. For days after that visit I would hear what seemed like an echo reverberating within the invisible walls of my being, "Listen to your body. Listen to your body. Listen to me. Hear me. Can you hear me?"

Normally neurotic, outspoken, irritable, frustrated, resentful, and full of anxiety, I remember questioning the unknown calm that slowly fell upon me. It was unfamiliar to look within, or to wonder why I did what I did, or why I felt what I felt. My purpose in life was to focus on what was going on outside of me, not to worry about what was going on inside of me. My priority was to ensure the people in my life were happy by tending to their needs. "You better listen to your body, Lisa, because your body is listening to you" simply did not compute.

Within a few years of that fateful doctor's visit, my husband and I separated. It marked the beginning of an excruciating detachment process that turned my life into an uncontrollable war zone. Listening to my body led me to gateways within I never knew existed. Honoring the paths I found as I learned to tune into the Self was no walk in the park. Awakening to the creator within meant confronting the zombie that existed within me as well. Coming face-to-face with the dual nature of my own existence was as crucifying as it was resurrecting.

The journey of a newly awakened soul is never easy. In fact, enlightenment oftentimes comes with a heavy price. Divorcing my husband meant putting an end to the codependent relationship I was in, but it did not mean I put an end to the codependent mind-set that helped create that dysfunctional marriage in the first place. This realization required a number of slaps in the face and kicks in the ass before I was able to make a substantial shift in my thinking process.

I am fortunate. I learned a lot about myself in the short time my ex-husband and I spent in therapy before we divorced. In my private counseling sessions I was diagnosed with depression, but was told that my depression was caused by codependency, and that my codependent mind-set was the result of being raised by two unrecovered adult children of alcoholics. I was as confused as I was hopeful about the possibility of being guided out of the swamp my mind and life had become. At that time the only understanding I had of the term "codependency" was linked to being married to an alcoholic, or drug addict. I could not immediately relate the term to my failing marriage. Eager to understand, I grabbed onto the term *codependent* and ran with it like a starving wolf might run with a bone.

Learning about codependency connected innumerable dots in my mind. Over time I began to understand how being raised by two unaware adult children of alcoholics created this Self-alienated being I had become. My marriage had become the emotional blueprinted copy of my childhood experiences, much like a template. I chased after my ex-husband's approval in the same way I had chased after my mother's approval. Feeling invisible had become a theme in my life. Seeing my Self as a codependent marked the beginning of a healing journey that would demand I clear out every crevice in my matted mind. At times the things that I discovered brought me to my knees.

Often I felt like I was training for the *Mental Olympics* as I struggled to understand that my mind was not my brain. Wrapping my consciousness around the idea that my brain and my mind were not one and the same was hellish to process. The moment I was able to intellectualize the concept that my brain was an organ, and that my mind was essentially reading the data that had been stored in the files of the brain, it brought order to the chaos my mental field had become. It was a much needed and welcomed moment of glory that helped light the torch at the end of what would be a very long tunnel.

Along my path I discovered that being raised by the unaware taught my brain to disconnect from my divine Self. Sadly, I also believed that whatever I was, I was unworthy. Being raised in a home that was intolerant of emotions brainwashed me to fear my feelings and to doubt the validity of my emotions as well. Never having my internal experiences validated caused me to become frozen and numb. Feeling my feelings terrified me. Disconnecting from them saved me. Disassociating from my internal experiences allowed me to survive excruciating alienation. As an adult I had no clue that my defense mechanisms, bizarre coping skills, and brainwashed, dysfunctional beliefs were actually the blueprints by which I had been designing my life.

As I moved forward on my journey, I began to understand why my life had been so unsatisfying, and what might happen if I never learned how to *confront my childhood programming*. I was hypersensitive to what was wrong with me, but had no mental construct for what might be right or good about me. I was aware of how to make others happy, yet had no psychological blueprint for how to make myself happy. I could tell you how others felt, but I was unable to connect to how I felt. I could feel empathy for strangers, yet had no compassion for my Self. I accepted other people's anger, although I experienced guilt and shame whenever I found myself slightly irritated. I could encourage someone else to go for his or her dreams, yet I felt undeserving of my own.

Realizations like these helped me uncover what was wrong. It was determination and desire, however, that allowed me to heal what needed to be undone. The book you are holding in your hands was designed to help you discover the dysfunctional thought patterns and belief systems that may be preventing you from living the life you deserve. The strategies you will learn will help you dig deep into your past, where the programs and beliefs reside. They will also assist you to assimilate and integrate them for the purpose of deep healing. As you progress through the material you will discover the purpose of reprogramming your mind from a higher state of consciousness. You will discover how to connect to the observer within, and how to harness the power of a highly aware mind.

If you are an adult child from a dysfunctional home, there is no doubt your unconscious belief systems could use a tune-up. If you are aware that you are unhappy, and know that your childhood brainwashing has impeded your ability to move forward, this book will help you get unstuck. If you believe your life is at a standstill, and you seek deeper Self-understanding, this book will help you uncover the unhealthy beliefs you need to discover in order to feel more fully integrated.

It is my hope that the strategies and insights you find in this book work like roadmaps to help you navigate your way towards true emotional freedom. The only way out is by going within. Dear One, *your* truth sets you free. It's not you—it's your programming.

Namaste...

FINDING THE COURAGE TO FACE THE REALITY THAT YOU WERE VICTIMIZED

Healing from this dysfunctional way of processing information about others and ourselves is not an easy task to accomplish. In fact, learning how to "observe" your own mind for the purpose of finding the junk information, in addition to needing to replace the old with some newer, healthier data, is just about as mind-twisting as it gets. Oftentimes you may feel overly intimidated by the old messages. You may also experience frustration as you learn to replace unhealthy codependent messages with new ones. Be gentle on yourself as you move forward. You are learning to be the ruler of your own kingdom, which of course is your mind.

It has been said that "as a man thinks, so is he." However, I believe a more concise and accurate quote might say something like, "Who a man has been brainwashed to think he is, so is he," or "What you see in your children, so will they be. Love-filled or love-less, a parent is the creator of their child's reality."

Because I understand how matted the codependent mind can become, I have created a list of Codependent Commandments that I believe will help you through the times when you are unsure of what new thought to put in place of an old codependent thought. On my road to recovery I oftentimes asked myself, "Am I doing this out of some old codependent belief system, or am I doing this because my true self wants to do this?"

Healthy, non-codependent adults who have been raised with uncon-ditionally loving parents are connected to their true self in ways code-pendent adults and children are not. A long time ago we dissociated with our emotions because we were brainwashed to believe our feelings did not matter, or because our psyches were too fragile to process the pain of our experiences when we were powerless to protect ourselves. Healing will require us to find the courage we need to face the fear of all those emotions we dissociated with so long ago. A huge part of our recovery is learning to embrace the idea that we really were victims, and that coming into psychological, emotional, and spiritual contact with this reality does not mean we are selfish, playing the victim, or are seek-ing pity. It simply means we are learning to appreciate our own experi-ences mind, body, and soul. It is one of the ways we get to feel "real."

CODEPENDENCY COMMANDMENTS

1. **Thou shall not have false gods before me**. I shall not honor someone else's opinion of me over my own divine opinion of me. My opinion of me must take precedence over someone else's opinion of me.

2. **Thou shall not lie**. I shall not say "yes" when I mean "no" and "no" when I mean "yes." I must learn to be my truth, to tell my truth, and to speak my truth even if others wish for me to lie.

3. **Thou shall rock the boat if necessary**. I shall not ignore or deny what I believe to be true for the sake of keeping others happy, calm, content, or happy.

4. **Thou shall not obsess about what others think about thee**. I shall teach my mind to focus on *my opinions* of my Self, career, relationships, success, body, recovery, and life choices.

5. **Thou shall not seek other's approval or permission to be**. I shall learn to seek the approval of my inner being first, and honor spirit's guidance even if what I wish for is not what others wish or want for me, them, or us.

6. **Thou shall learn to honor the temple of thy divine spirit.** I shall learn to treat my physical body as the divine extension of god/source that it is. I shall learn to thank my heart, liver, kidneys, pancreas, intestines, skin, eyes, ears, mouth, throat,

and chakra system for allowing my spirit the opportunity to experience my spiritual journey through this divine physical apparatus—my divine temple.

7. **Thou shall learn to trust anxiety**. I shall learn to use anxiety as an indicator that my thoughts, or my body, are not in alignment with my true destiny. I shall learn to trust when I do not feel well around others as a sign that I may be in the company of people who do not resonate with my spirit's being-ness. I shall trust when I feel like someone has punched me in the gut. On a vibrational (emotional and spiritual) level they probably have wounded me. I will use this guidance to help me navigate throughout my life, and learn to avoid people who are insensitive, cruel, manipulative, judgmental, or unkind.

8. **Thou shall seek contentment and stillness and avoid chaos, unpredictability, indifference, or abuse**. I shall seek to remove myself from situations, conversations, stories, images, and people who elicit tension, unhappiness, anger, or depression in me. I shall learn to take responsibility for my gut reactions, and extract myself from situations rather than contribute to ones that cause my being to be out of alignment with contentment.

9. **Thou shall learn to accept others have rights to their own reality of thee, even if their reality is faulty, hurtful, discouraging, disapproving, shameful, and wrong**. I shall learn to accept that I have no right to control how other people think, feel, and/or behave. I shall learn to honor how others feel, rather than engage in trying to change how they feel. I shall learn to walk away from people who fail to see the good in me.

10. **Thou shall not judge thy neighbor**. I shall learn to turn the cheek and walk away rather than to contribute to the negative vibration of judgment of others. I shall learn to bless all that is, and to navigate my thoughts, actions, and intentions according to what my spirit discerns as either in alignment with my divine being or out of alignment with my divine being.

RECOVERY IS POSSIBLE

Unlike the physical body, spirit is ageless, limitless, and immortal. It is not possible to destroy the energy that is the sum of the vibrational energetic beings we are at our core. Therefore, it is possible for an individual to begin the resuscitation of one's spirit at any time. As long as there is a beating heart, a thinking mind, and oxygen flowing through one's bloodstream, spiritual resurrection is possible. I mention this only because so often I have heard clients say things like, "It is probably too late for me to figure this all out," or "I have been in recovery programs for thirty years and I still feel like I am where I was when I started."

All of these statements are true and valid, but they do not represent an absolute. It is *irrelevant* the amount of *time* one spends seeking to be healed. The only thing relevant is how committed, disciplined, and persistent one is to one's ultimate victory over the dysfunctional patterning that is held within the mind. Programs are just patterns of thoughts that have been recycled over and over. When one applies discipline to the concept of healing the programs that no longer serve their higher good, true healing can occur.

If you were taught that your feelings were unimportant as a child, and if that belief was proven to be true through repetition and observation in your home, you may be unaware of how that limiting belief is being played out in your adult life today. Once a thought is accepted as truth, the mind does not question its validity. Lifetimes are built upon ideas that are created in childhood, when one is innocent and impressionable.

We are unaware that much of our pain may be the result of a childhood programming—patterns of thought—and so we do not know to scan the mind like one would an x-ray for the broken thought processes causing our pain.

Thought Doctors

If thoughts were bones, it would be simple to figure out what was wrong. A codependent, disempowering, victim mentality-littered thought process would be fairly easy to see, diagnose, and treat. If we wished to be validated, but used the counterproductive codependent thought process to guilt others as a way to produce validation from them, it would be easy to see that crack in one of our bones. We would then go to a Thought Doctor, who would instruct us perhaps like this:

"Go home and look at this thought process. I want you to understand that you are enough, and you no longer need to stomp your feet to gain validation. The truth is you are enough and you always were. Now, if you invited ninety-seven of your teenage daughter's friends to your home for a pool party, that is something YOU chose to do because YOU wanted to, because YOU were trying to find a way to express your love for your daughter. However, it is unfair, manipulative, counterproductive, sneaky, and controlling of you to berate your daughter for weeks on end for not speaking, and acting like she does not appreciate you enough for all that you do for her. It is malicious of you to hang your actions over her head because she did not publicly announce at the party how grateful she was to her mom for all she has ever done for her, including throwing her a pool party for ninety-seven teenagers. Dear One, go home, and learn this lesson so you can stop recycling the same type of emotional, codependent, abusive, power-over-communication tactics your mother and father used on you. Then and only then will the pain in your body begin to fade. Dear One, when you finally accept that you are and always were enough, and that the only thing that prevented you from feeling worthy were the patterns of thoughts you were conditioned to think, then you will finally find your way to Self-love. Then and only then will you feel validated as a divine *Being*. At this time you will also begin learning how to be more naturally accepting, loving, understanding, forgiving, and nurturing towards your family. And as you open up to your own worth, you will quite naturally begin pouring that love and that light onto those around you. Dear One, the games stop, and souls recover. Remember to drink plenty of fluids and to avoid alcohol, caffeine, and white flour. Call me in a week and let me know how well you are doing then."

CHILDREN ARE NOT TAUGHT HOW TO THINK IN A HEALTHY WAY

We are not taught to think about the way we think. We are not taught to question why we do what we do. Most of us just react to whatever data shows up in our mental field, and never stop to question what is showing up. If we fear making a decision about a relationship we are in, we do not routinely question why we are afraid of making a decision. Most of us worry about making a decision, then feel the physical response to that fear in our bodies as stress, and eventually suffer from anxiety-related issues. We fail to recognize what this habit of thought is costing us in our adult lives. If we understood that many of us fear making decisions because there is a template in our mind that has taught us that what we feel is insignificant, we would then understand why we find ourselves worrying about making decisions.

When we understand that the way we think is the result of what we observed and not the product of being taught how to think in a healthy way, it becomes easier to understand the concept that the subconscious mind is essentially a computer that has been downloaded with a specific computer language. Just like computers, which are subject to what data and programs are downloaded into its motherboard by a programmer, children's innocent, virgin minds are no different. Children learn how to process the world by observing the people around them. Through consistency and observations, children are brainwashed to believe what their caretakers believe. In this way, a child's mind is truly not his/her own. Instead, the way a child processes information, which includes data he/she experiences in relation to the Self, healthy or not, is the handiwork of programmers.

Tremendous self-doubt is a characteristic of an adult child who has grown up in a dysfunctional home that was void of authentic love, communication, and validation. If your brain holds templates that have taught you that what you need is insignificant, then it will be almost impossible for you to make healthy choices on your own behalf until this template is confronted and dismantled. You may have been programmed to be successful at a career, but you may have been taught that your emotions are insignificant. In this case, you might be someone who is highly functional at work, but you may feel insecure in your personal relationships. How you behave in any given situation as an adult will always be the result of the templates that have been created by your childhood programming.

The 12 Keys to Recovery are designed to help you foster new ideas concerning your perception of Self. If you do not believe you possess the power to change, it is my hope and intention to help you shift out of that victim-like posture and into a possibly more victorious perception of Self. Just like any thought process that has been instilled in your mind, it will take time, patience, and repetition to override the patterns that are already within your subconscious mind.

As you discipline yourself to the practices outlined in this book, you will begin to flourish in ways you could have never imagined. As veils begin to lift from your eyes, the colors in nature will seem brighter and more illumined. You might begin to notice that you sleep more soundly and feel lighter in your being. Your skin tone may improve, along with your hair and nails. Your digestive system may begin to become more regulated, and brain fog may disappear completely. You may notice that your relationships with others are improving, or that some relationships begin fading away. You may notice a sudden desire to organize your closets and drawers. You may discover a sudden urge to save money and to take better care of your car. All of these new and exciting acts of Self Responsibility are a byproduct of taking more responsibility for what you think, say, and do.

In time you will happily discover that one day it will be second nature for you:

- to desire healthy life experiences
- to desire healthy, Self-responsible friends and partners
- to tell the truth even when it chances hurting someone else's feelings
- to say no when you mean no, and yes when you mean yes
- to focus more on what you do want rather than on what you don't want
- to practice personal development techniques each and every day
- to honor your emotions
- to honor other people's emotions even if they differ from yours
- to detach from and avoid toxic relationships, conversations, experiences, and people
- to no longer judge yourself or others harshly
- to be more Self-loving and more loving to others
- to give without the intent to manipulate validation out of others
- to speak from a position of Self-empowerment rather than the victim plane
- to accept when others dislike you, without being crushed by their opinions
- to respect differing viewpoints
- to act on your own desires

- to manifest more fulfilling life experiences
- to nurture Self
- to ask Self what you need to feel more peaceful right now
- to take responsibility for nurturing, feeding, and supporting the Self
- to search your own heart for healthy ways to improve your mental and emotional state
- to act upon, rather than react to, situations, others, conversations, and thoughts
- to go no contact with negative others if necessary
- to be calm and rational when explaining how you feel
- to be more willing to speak about how you feel
- to hold others accountable for how they treat you
- to be unattached to outcomes
- to accept that you have no right to expect others to change so you can be more comfortable in this lifetime
- to accept that it is up to you to parent yourself appropriately if you need to
- to say "I am sorry" when you have been insensitive or unkind
- to expect others to mean it when they say "I am sorry"
- to be willing and able to enforce a boundary with an action step if a set boundary has been violated
- to seek things in your environment that please your inner being
- to seek communion with your inner being before you seek unions with others
- to come to rely on the guidance of Self for direction rather than seek direction from others
- to know beyond a shadow of a doubt you are enough, always have been, and always will be

THE TWELVE KEYS
TO RECOVERY

1. Beyond Desire There Is Humility and the Hidden Power of *Asking*

You must be humble enough to be asking for help in order to receive that which you hear your mind wishing for. The greater your desire to change, the quicker and easier your recovery will be. Asking is the first step. As it is written in ancient teachings, "Ask and it is given," "Seek and ye shall find," "Knock and the door opens," "When the student is ready, the teacher appears."

If you are not humble enough to ask *how to* heal and recover, you cannot receive the guidance and instructions you seek. It is also written, "Only the meek and humble shall inherit the kingdom of Heaven."

Heaven is your birthright, and it is just a few ironed-out dank thought processes away. As you recover you will begin to become faintly aware of what it feels like to honor Self, and experience sudden, unexpected moments of emotional freedom and bliss. Eventually as you continue on this path of healing and enlightenment, your being will become accustomed to lengthier moments of contentment. If you stay committed to your path, you will discover that heaven was with you all the while, and that it was only when you were not believing in Self (living through the old subconscious prism) that chaos was at your front door.

It is important to understand the concept of asking. When we ask for help and we receive it, we feel validated. But when someone muscles onto our territory, and perhaps takes over a task that they presume is too difficult for us, from the outside looking in it would seem as if in both cases we were receiving help. In reality, however, only when we ask for the help can we appreciate what we receive. It is only when we ask for instruction that we learn. Anything short of learning could be considered enabling. For this reason it is not entirely effective to help drug addicts, alcoholics, or people who we know are in difficult situations they seem to be contributing to. Until that person asks for help, they will not be emotionally ready to receive the help, or benefit from it.

Asking for clarity, healing, and help is linked to the desire to experience a more pleasurable life experience. If you simply desire a healthier life without asking how or what you can do to actually create a better life, it will leave you feeling stuck. When you couple your desire for change with questions like "What needs to change in my life in order for me to experience contentment and peace?" or "What is it that I need to change in order to create a different life experience?" it is then that you are in the optimal emotional and mental space to shift.

Humility is a big part of this process, if not the cornerstone. Why? Humility allows your ego to lessen its grasp on your ability to look within. In spite of how horrific our life experiences may have been, the universe can only respond to our vibrational frequencies in the NOW. The universe is indifferent. It keeps no record of wrong or right, and knows nothing about good or bad. The universe aligns us with situations, circumstances, ideas, others, and experiences that mimic our vibrational frequencies. If you are waiting for the universe to match you up with a partner who can love you unconditionally, but you have not yet learned to unconditionally love the Self, you are wasting your precious time.

Desire is a key to healing, only when coupled with *asking* with an open heart. We've all heard the phrase, "God helps those who help themselves." This phrase is in fact true, even if you do not believe in God. Why? In essence you are the God of your reality. You are the creator of all that is happening in your life. And although that may be really tough to swallow, I truly hope your curiosity has been sparked. It is my desire that you keep an open mind as you move forward with this book. I ask that you imagine that what you are reading is in fact true, and how your life might change if it is.

God does help those who help themselves, because you are the God within. When you help yourself, you also discover how to heal your life.

2. Mention Your Intention

Most people are unintentional with their thoughts, feelings, and actions. Most of us are reactive and do not even realize it. We have these belief systems that were programmed into us long ago, and when we hit adolescence we go out into the world operating out of this "standard operating system" our caretakers downloaded into us when we were innocent, powerless creatures. If our fathers blew up when they got frustrated over small tasks, so do we, or we attract people who blow up when they become frustrated. If our mothers catered to our fathers and ignored their own emotions, often we do the same in our own relationships or attract people we tend to cater to, because we may be unaware we have been brainwashed to ignore our feelings, and to do everything possible to avoid making others upset.

To truly heal you must be willing to live intentionally through thought, word, and deed. Invoking this practice allows you to slip into the driver's seat of your own life. You learn what it feels like to be hopeful and empowered. You slowly learn to tap into your Godlike ability to steer your own life. When you move out of reactive living and into living with intention, you literally invoke the same energies that created this universe. How exciting is that?

- You must intend to heal.
- You must see yourself healed.
- You must intend to one day finally be free of all the old childhood programming.
- You must intend to be vigilant and tend to the garden that is your mind like a dedicated gardener.
- You must intend to seek out the destructive patterns and confront them head-on.
- You must intend to be on a mission to find the exact dysfunctional thoughts/programs that are rolling around in your subconscious/conscious mind.

3. Discipline and Win

The dysfunctional roots in your mind are deep, and only discipline, desire/humility, and intention can create effective change. Discipline is what you will need to practice to heal completely. Imagine if you chose to do three things every day for the next ten years. Imagine how much energy that would create in the direction of the intentions you were working on. Imagine how far you would get if you disciplined yourself in the art of Self-study. Imagine if, no matter what was happening in your life, you disciplined yourself to the point where each and every day, your agenda was to scan your mental field for thoughts that represented old programming for the purpose of dissolving them through Self-awareness. Imagine becoming so conscious that in a moment of weakness, when you heard yourself criticize someone else, immediately following that thought you heard your mind say, "That's not me. I do not wish to be critical of others. That thought represents an old template. My mother was overly critical of me when I was younger, which taught me to be critical of my Self and of others. That thought is not mine. I can let it go. I actually love people, and my Self."

Discipline is an art and it can be self-taught. If you lack discipline, that is probably because the people who raised you lacked discipline. Your parents may have been disciplined with their career, but lacked discipline when it came to alcohol, verbal abuse, personal health, hygiene, or their temperament. The kind of discipline I am referring to is found through supreme Self-accountability. If you want to heal your life, you can, but you will need tools to help you achieve this goal. You can have an amazing life, but if you are waiting for your life to just change or shift all on its own, it cannot. Nothing changes until something changes. Your vibrational frequency was set a long time ago, when you were innocent, powerless, and unaware, and until you change your emotional set point, your life will not change much at all. The power to heal and to manifest abundance truly is within your reach, and this book was designed to be the roadmap you need to help you achieve your dreams.

4. Detachment Versus Enmeshment

Detaching from our emotions allows us to objectify our emotions like we would a specimen on a microscopic slide. YOU ARE NOT YOUR EMOTIONS. Your emotions are a byproduct of how you think, and how you think is the result of what you experienced as a child. YOU at your core are perfect, minus the dysfunctional thoughts, ideas, and beliefs you were taught to believe about your Self.

Modern psychology tells us that our emotions come from our thoughts. Yes, that is true, but this is not where this train ends, or should end. In fact, consciousness has the ability to question its reality. Human beings can and should think about the way they think. Most of us have been duped into believing that we have no choice when it comes to what shows up in our mental fields. Nothing could be further from the truth. I can feel rage and think about wanting to lash out at the person who just cut me off on the highway. But I can also think about that emotional reaction, and choose not to react to the rage. I can think about why I fear leaving my abusive boyfriend, and still choose to leave him anyway, in spite of the fact that I have been programmed to doubt my decisions, as well as my right to live an abundant life.

Children raised by dysfunctional caretakers are brainwashed to believe faulty ideas about the Self and others. Perhaps the most debilitating unconscious, brainwashed belief is the "I am not enough" belief. When children are ignored, beaten, minimized, and criticized, they are being brainwashed to presume that they—whoever "they" are—are not enough. This aching sense of *I am not enough* permeates every thought, spoken or unspoken, in our adult lives. When we meet new people, unconsciously we sense the ghost that whispers, "You are not enough." Some of us develop what appear to be tough skins, while others of us come off as super needy and attached. But beneath both outward demeanors is the undercurrent that weeps silently, "I am not enough. I can't be enough, because not even my own parents thought I was enough."

When we carry with us this heavy wound, we tend to enmesh with our pain rather than objectify it. When we enmesh with our pain, our goal becomes to avoid deeper pain at all costs. Because we have not been permitted to achieve the much needed psychological milestone of feeling "seen" by our caretakers, we presume that if we can somehow find a way to feel "seen" by another, all of our woes will disappear, and we will finally feel *enough*. Then finally we believe we will be happy.

A key to healing is being able to detach from your emotions so that you can inspect them for the purpose of understanding where the pain is actually coming from, much like you would palpate your leg to isolate a leg pain. Yes, you feel the pain in your leg, but you do not enmesh with the pain. Instead your intention is to understand where it is coming from. And so, part of your investigation will include a personal exam of the pain for the purpose of understanding its root cause so you can address the pain appropriately.

Emotions are tricky because we have not been taught to objectify our feelings. Instead we are stuck in reactive states of behavior, driven by an unconscious need to feel seen, validated, appreciated, and loved by others. And until we finally sit down and do what needs to be done to learn how to master the way we think, we stay like sheep and live outside of our own bodies, in search of a God to follow, rather than learning how to step into the role of God within.

5. Find the Higher Mind

Your brain cannot think. Your brain holds thoughts, beliefs, and thought processes that were downloaded into your mind when you were young. The brain is coded with certain reflexes, like the pain-versus-pleasure principle, and the fear of drowning. The brain is designed to alert you to possible threats. The brain, however, relies very much on your emotional body to help it decipher what is threatening to you. For instance, in the case of war veterans who have experienced fear immediately after hearing a loud blast, the brain will be wired to respond with the flight or fight response in reaction to hearing a sudden loud noise even when not in battle. I believe the brain is simply trying to protect us when we experience posttraumatic stress responses.

If every time you told your parents how you felt when you were a small child you were hit, criticized, or ignored, you may feel great fear today as an adult whenever you wish to express a concern you may be having. Your body will respond in similar ways as it did when you were a child, but as an adult you may not understand the connection. You may be wondering, "I own a company, and I have a number of employees. I am successful, and yet whenever I feel like I need to confront someone about something uncomfortable, I tend to feel overwhelmed."

Until we take the time to really dig into our pasts to discover the wiring that has been created in situations like the one above, we are doomed to repeat our pasts. We are doomed only because we remain asleep, like sheep, rather than awaken to our true potential. Understanding the three distinct aspects of the mind will help you move along the healing journey, because the more you understand the tool you use to create your life, the better you will become at operating your life.

Your mind is comprised of three very distinct aspects.

- The Subconscious Mind. Here you store all your secret wishes, dreams, talents, and goals as well as all of your learned fears, doubts, guilt, rage, shame, the fear of not ever being enough, and so on. In the subconscious mind exists the tug of war between the real you and the false you others brainwashed you to believe you are. Emotions are created in this realm. This plane represents 95 percent of the total mind. You can think about this realm as the "feeling" realm.
- The Conscious Mind. This aspect of the mind thinks about the feelings, ideas, fears, beliefs that rise up out of the subconscious mind. It is a reactive center as opposed to a feeling center. It represents 5 percent of the total mind. You can think of this realm as the "thinking" realm.
- The Higher Conscious Mind. This realm is where a mind gets to question the ideas and emotions that are surfacing on the floors below it. From this realm we get to practice non-attachment. From this space we understand that we were always

- 20 -

enough. Through the powers of the higher mind we are able to definitively separate our true divine nature from thoughts and emotions that are the product of childhood templates created within our subconscious mind when we were powerless to challenge them. From this realm we discover the authentic meaning of free will. We learn to understand what it means to be the ultimate creator and/or alchemist of our quantum nature. This is the realm in which we discover the power of focus and our ability to decide what thoughts we wish to entertain. The higher conscious mind is infinitely expansive.

Healing will require us to work through the lower aspects of the mind, which have been corrupted by the repetitious, dysfunctional, spiritual representations of the authorities in our lives, so that we can effectively connect to and nurture the higher realms of consciousness. When we arrive at this realm, from here we make decisions based on Self-love. We no longer judge, criticize, bash, doubt, shame, or guilt Self or others. We live from the "I Am" perspective and allow all others to take responsibility for their own actions, living our lives according to our own spiritual and emotional guidance, without compromising our state of harmony.

Most human beings are not conscious. A mind that has not questioned its contents can never really know if what it is thinking is the product of his own creation or the byproduct of someone else's thought processes and beliefs. The contents of a child's mind are the result of his/her childhood programming. Therefore, until the mind of the child (subconscious mind) is scrutinized by the soul in possession of that mind, the being can never really be certain that the thoughts he/she thinks belong to them or are the consequences of the minds who raised them.

Understanding the mind is a tool you can use to help you detach from your programming and gain some sense of control over what is currently happening in your mind, body, and life. All human beings hold within them the potential to increase their level of Self-awareness and to expand their consciousness. If you live in fear, you are not basking in the knowing that you are enough, always were, and always will be. You may be stuck in a false belief, created in childhood, that has you believing in a false premise. Although your feet are not stapled to the floor, you may in fact feel frozen. You may feel powerless and as if you have no choices. By now I hope you are beginning to understand that these feelings are the result of your childhood programming, that you have yet learned how to uncover, detach from, investigate, objectify, organize, and override.

6. Nudge the Judge

Emotional freedom requires us to nudge the judge from the nonphysical throne that exists in the center of our minds, hearts, and bodies. The judge's voice is an echo that has been recorded into each and every cell of the emotional body. Although the cells that created your two-year-old body have long gone, still in the invisible halls of the cellular structures that create and envelop your totality lives the echo of the judge's voice whispering, "You are not enough." This echoing must be silenced, and only the higher conscious aspect of you can nudge that judge from your RIGHTFUL place as ruler over the quantum kingdom that represents the total being you are!

When we are children, we are in a dream state. We are unaware we are unaware. We do not know that deep within our subconscious mind every word the authorities in our lives speak, and every perceived flaw we see being reflected back to us through their eyes, will be downloaded onto a template that will act as the framework for our future lives. If our parents were dead to themselves, we will presume that that emptiness represents some aspect of us. We will see that lack of love in their eyes, and presume we are unworthy of love, because we do not see love being reflected back to us. This feeling of unworthiness will then act like an echo that regardless of how many times the cells in our bodies die and regenerate will remain.

The judge we need to nudge is part of the template that was created so long ago. And it is only through the power of awareness that we get to deconstruct that template, as well as replace it with a healthier one. The process of healing is truly a process. It will take time, patience, determination, and commitment to fine-tune your ability to focus. The human mind is habitual. If you have thought negative, Self-defeating thoughts for many years, it will take you time to acknowledge them, rather than react to them. But if you stay on track, ultimately you will learn what it is to own your own mind.

7. Acceptance Leads to Transcendence

Acceptance just may be the most undervalued tool in a human being's psychological tool belt. Regardless of whatever is happening in our lives, the reality is it's happening. What most of us do not realize is that very often we do not accept what is happening in the moment, even though it is in fact happening. When a wife finds lipstick on her husband's collar, she may choose to ignore what she sees. Deeper, she may choose to ignore the flight or fight response she feels standing there holding his shirt in her hands. It is unhealthy not to accept what is happening in the now. Not accepting what is happening in the now causes the brain to malfunction. It is healthier to learn how to integrate the emotions that show up in any given moment, and later to decide what you want to do about the situation that has been presented. When we are children, the ability to dissociate from our bodies helped us survive. In the case of sexual abuse, when a child is molested or raped, the brain goes into survival mode and shunts the emotional experience. The ability to do so acts like a psychological safety net. Although the emotional experience has been stored in the subconscious mind, the mind has the ability to protect the psyche from being overwhelmed.

On the healing journey it will be essential that you learn to feel your emotions as they show up in your everyday experiences. However, severe childhood trauma should be dealt with in the company of a trained professional. If at any time you feel like your memories are too much for you to handle, I suggest you simply ask the brain to store the information until you feel like you are in a setting that will allow you to feel more comfortable as you attempt to integrate them.

Emotions are stored energy. The key is to learn how to drop the mind as you at same time allow these energies to simply filter through your energetic (chakra) system. Because we have learned to attach meanings to our feelings, our minds have been programmed to fear what we feel. In reality, we have already experienced whatever has happened in the present moment. The next step is to learn how to allow the emotions that naturally show up when we are presented with a difficult situation to filter through our chakra system like water flows through cheese-cloth, without attaching negative connotations to the emotions.

Have a flat tire? Accept it, and decide how to get back into the flow of abundant momentum again.

Have a headache and you are fifteen minutes late to work? Accept it, and decide how you can get back into alignment with your upcoming schedule for the day.

Angry at your friend because she just passed a really sarcastic comment your way? Accept that you feel angry. Trust that your anger is valid and is trying to help you realize you need a boundary to protect you from her comments in the future. Or perhaps her comment activated an un-healed code deep within you that needs to be consciously worked on.

Decide what you want to do about your friend's comment.

- Do you wish to ask her, "Why would you say something like that?"
- Do you want to say, "Excuse me, but I am suddenly feeling a little nauseous, and I want to go home"?
- Do you wish to begin breaking ties with her?

Acceptance does not imply that you like or agree with what is happening in the moment. Acceptance is the way you stay out of resisting the desired big picture. You want ease, so in order to experience ease, you must seek ways to move forward toward the broader goal you wish to experience in your life.

If you are an abused adult child, you may have been taught to fear your emotions rather than to validate them. This absolutely must be corrected in order to heal completely.

8. Honor Self More

When you *feel* a feeling—honor it. This does not imply that when we get cut off on the highway and we feel rage due to suddenly finding ourselves in fear of possibly being involved in a car accident, we chase the driver down and curse him/her out. It means that when we feel the rage, we accept it and we honor it. We allow it to surface without REACTING to it. Honoring a feeling happens in the conscious realm, without REACTING to it detached from the big picture we are trying to create in our lives.

The Self does not ooze out of your body and sit across from you at your kitchen table to discuss how you are feeling. Your Self speaks to you through your emotional body. It is helpful to understand that the trinity is YOU. You are the body, the mind, and the spirit (soul/Self). Your body is a consequence of this time-space reality we call the earthly experience. To play on planet Earth, you need a body that is equipped with a central nervous system and central computer. Within your divine, magical, electrical suit is housed your most divine aspect of you—your Self. The body truly is your temple. You must see clearly that although your body is your temple, your mind or your central command station may be corrupt. Your body will never lie to you because it is connected to the universe through its electrical system. Your heart beats, and so does the earth. Your body goes through cycles, just as the earth does. Your body experiences seasons very similarly to planet Earth. Your emotional body is divine, and when you learn to trust its guidance, you are literally listening to your inner guide seeking to escort you away from pain, and toward more fulfilling life experiences. You, Dear One, have simply been brainwashed to mistrust the cues from the divine Self. This book has been created to help you get back on track and stay on course so you can merge with the light within you.

9. Action Versus Reaction

Codependents, ACoAs, (adult children of alcoholics) and love addicts react to everything. We are like puppets on strings, and because we have *not* been taught to think appropriately, because we have been forced to grow up in states of survival, we do not have the strong, conditioned emotional muscles needed to *think* rather than *react*. In addition, because we have been taught to overreact to even the tiniest drops of milk spilling onto the floor, our subconscious minds run programs similar to the ones the authorities in our lives taught us.

If your parents reacted rather than thought about how they were feeling, then you have been brainwashed to react to and enmesh with your emotions. Like a horse that is being led by his nose with a carrot, you may be living your life following your emotions, rather than learning how to master your emotions. Learning to see this trait in yourself is essential on your healing path. When you are able to see this trait in yourself, then you are in a position to take action to change.

10.　Victor = Victim No More

Emotional freedom will require you to refuse to posture yourself as a victim EVER again. When you hear your mind whining, *Woe is me*, you must THINK and ACT from higher realms of consciousness.

Woe is me posturing is a learned dysfunctional behavior. Alcoholics, narcissists, and emotionally self-absorbed beings teach their children how to think, act, and feel like victims. Because alcoholics, narcissists, abusers, and addicts do not take responsibility for their actions, the children of such individuals are void of proper emotional and intellectual coping skills. Worse, we the innocent children of the Self-absorbed repeat our caretakers' programming, in spite of how often we hear ourselves wishing we were different.

Have you ever been in the process of doing something you really did not want to be doing, and felt powerless to change what you were doing? Perhaps you were screaming at your children the way your parents screamed at you, and although you could hear some higher aspect of you begging you to stop, you couldn't. I believe this is because the brain can only play with the tools that are in the shed. If the only pattern you have in your mind that is linked to frustration is screaming, then that is the only thing the brain can react with. If you have never spent the time to rewire the landscape of your brain for a different reaction to the emotion of frustration, your brain will be powerless to act in any other way, until you choose to reframe how you perceive and react to the emotion of frustration.

A key to your recovery lies in your willingness to accept dominion over the landscape of your own mind. Within you lives a victor who has only been taught he/she is a victim. These tools will help you shift and step into your true role as leader of your own life. Along this road you will discover that thinking requires work, and it is my hope that you are as excited as I am about the endless potential an awakened human mind holds.

11.   Commit Without Limit

A golden key to recovery is found in taking total accountability for every thought, spoken or unspoken, as well as any action witnessed by others or not. Committing to emotional freedom implies that we do not accept limits when it comes to how far we are willing to go to ensure we are one day free of the chains of bondage our family of origins reinforced.

We commit to taking total responsibility for the happenings in our mind, knowing that through the proper attention to focus we can shift our perceptions in any moment. Even if the world is falling apart around us, we can, even in those moments, choose to place our third eye's attention on any thought, idea, or wish we desire that affords us the opportunity to find balance at that point in time.

No longer are our moods dictated by the moods, thoughts, sarcasm, jealousies, rage, anger, or opinions of others. We have learned to honor the true ruler of the temple that is our Self, which is our *I Am* presence.

The *I Am* presence is likened to a jug that holds a gallon of milk. Just as without the jug there is no ability to manage or control the flow of milk, without the *I Am* presence (higher aspect of Self), there is little control or flow of focused attention. In this recovery program we will be learning how to control the flow of our attention for the purpose of stepping into our true roles as rulers over our own kingdom, which represents the trinity beings we are—mind, body, and spirit.

12. Surrender Is the Mender

To fight, deny, split off from, hide from, ignore, shame, hate, and/or fear ANY aspect of us that is dark is like ignoring a gangrenous toe. We can do it, but eventually not taking responsibility for the aspect of us that is not so attractive will consume us completely.

Surrendering to the shadows within us allows for light to move into those shadows. Just as surrendering to the fact that we have a gangrenous toe allows us to seek and get help for our infection and allows healing to finally begin. When we surrender, we do not do so under the assumptions that we must like where we are, or what we have done, or what we have experienced in our lifetime. Just as when surrendering to the reality that we have a gangrenous toe does not mean we enjoy or like the fact that we have a gangrenous toe, it simply implies that we understand *it is what it is, it was what it was,* and *we are where we are.*

It is quite challenging to accept that we are on divorce number three from another narcissist, or that one of our children is a drug addict. It can be excruciating to take honest inventories of our lives. On my own healing journey, there were many times what I discovered about myself made me want to stay in bed for a lifetime. There are ghosts from the past we need to face, battle, and overcome. This journey is a lonely one, because the truth is no one can do your healing for you. No one can look into the pockets of pain you possess and heal your wounds but you. Regardless of how many books you read or therapists you seek, the ultimate truth is only YOU can heal YOU. The really fabulous news is,

YOU CAN. You can heal your life. You can overcome your childhood programming. You can become the victor of your life. You can reframe, shift, awaken, expand, love, laugh, and be free. You can because all you need to do so has been coded into your godlike DNA.

It is time to awaken to your potential, Dear One. It is time to learn how to use your mind, your emotions, and your vibrations to your advantage. It is time to step into your rightful place as the creator or your own new, deliberate reality!

Resisting anything is like adding logs to a fire. The energy of resistance is what fuels that which we resist, which causes it to persist.

It is true; that which we resist, persists. However, it is also true that "persistence is to the character of man as carbon is to steel" (Napoleon Hill).

To gain control over anything, one must persist until that gain is had. To recover from the mind-twisting woes that only a child who has grown up in a dysfunctional home could ever fathom requires one to persist through the bumps, twists, and deep valleys the road to recovery involves. There is no question in my mind that roads to recovery are not fun. They are not scenic in the sense that the impressions that show up in the windows of our minds have anything at all to do with pretty blue fairies, gumdrops, and lemon drops. Recovery is a grueling process, and will absolutely test the will, as well as challenge the desire of the one in search of their healing.

Resisting any of the 12 Keys to Recovery is to impress the mind with the notion that it is not possible to conquer the gain at hand. Many ACoAs, codependents, love addicts, alcoholics, as well as any being who is battling an addiction of any kind struggle with the discipline required to master the skill of "scanning the mind" for dysfunctional thought patterns. I have encountered more than one client who began coaching because he/she thought I had some magic pill they could swallow that would allow all their dysfunctional data to disintegrate. While it is of tremendous value to have someone like me model for a client how to scan the mind for dysfunctional patterns of thought, only the one seeking the healing can open the doors that need to be opened within the invisible halls of their emotional, mental, and physical bodies. I can knock, but it is up to the individual to, day in and day out, open the doors that need to be opened.

If you are ready to take full responsibility for your recovery process, then this book of strategies will serve you, Dear One. If you are not ready, and you resist any of the Keys to Recovery, while you may benefit to some degree if you attempt them at all, your recovery will be limited to the extent you hold back from cleaning the house that is the trinity you are—mind, body, and soul.

The recovery processes offered in this book are designed under one premise—that each and every being holds within them the absolute creative power to change their destinies. These strategies have been designed to empower and respect the divine being you are at your core. It has been founded on principles that respect the innocent child victim you once were, while at the same time, it helps you to formulate deeper truths about Self that are reflective of your true godlike personal power.

UNIQUE CHALLENGES OF EMOTIONALLY ABUSED ADULT CHILDREN FROM DYSFUNCTIONAL HOMES

Adult children from dysfunctional homes suffer from an array of emotional and cognitive issues. Emotions drive cognition and ultimately help us decide what actions and decisions we choose as adults. Children raised by parents who condition them to fear, deny, repress, disown, and hate their emotions are stunted not only emotionally but cognitively as well. In order to think well and in alignment with what is best for the individual, one must be able to process information from non-emotional and more rational conscious realms. Children from dysfunctional homes who have been taught to fear their feelings are rooted to moments of childhood trauma because they have not been permitted to express the emotional energy created by the trauma. Thus, there is no sense of resolution.

In order to be able to process information through resolution, there needs to be ordered thought processes in place for resolve and growth to occur. In the case of children born to dysfunctional parents when there is no order, structure, or conflict resolution of emotions and/or events, minds get stuck in the emotional centers of the brain. Because children born into chaos are powerless and are forced to exist in constant states of survival, neural wiring to the prefrontal lobe, which is necessary for higher states of reasoning, is immature at best.

Children are powerless and they know it. For those of us who were raised by parents who abused their power over us and exploited their authority whether through criticism, beatings, or any form of abuse, knowing we were powerless forced us to disengage from our emotions. For many reasons we had to.

- *If when we were terrified we acted like we were terrified, many of us knew that whatever abuse was occurring at the time would probably only get worse if we dared express ourselves.*
- *If when we were sad we expressed our sadness, many of us understood we would only get chastised for daring to express that emotion.*
- *If when we were angry we actually dared tell our mother or father we were angry, many of us knew we would be shamed for expressing that anger, or our caretakers would try to make us feel guilty for daring to tell our truth.*
- *If when we needed something and we dared ask for it, many of us knew that we would be labeled selfish for actually daring to want something other than what our caretakers thought we deserved.*
- *If when we were sick we dared act like we were sick, many of us were labeled drama queens, actors, or were treated with indifference. Because it hurt less to keep how we felt to ourselves, we did, and in so doing reinforced our unhealthy detachment to our right to feel what we were feeling.*

The challenges of adult children from dysfunctional homes are many. But that is not where our stories end. In fact, this is where many of our stories finally get to begin.

When we get to points in our lives where we are experiencing the sense that we have hit rock bottom, it is then that we tend to begin asking the right types of questions. Hitting rock bottom implies that we are done trying to get others to:

- Validate us
- Approve of us
- Help us feel real
- Tell us we are worthy
- Tell us we are enough
- See us
- Hear us
- Guide our lives
- Take responsibility for our happiness
- Take responsibility for our unhappiness
- Complete us
- Take care of us financially
- Take care of us emotionally
- Give our life meaning and purpose

When we hit rock bottom, and we feel completely exhausted by the inept ways in which we have tried to cope with the stressors in our lives, it is then that we find ourselves humbled by the idea that perhaps we need some real help to figure out what the hell it is we are doing wrong.

The Great Thing About Hitting Rock Bottom

The Quantum Advantage

There are many unappreciated advantages about hitting rock bottom. On a quantum level, it is when we are in the pits of despair that we are highly emotional. Deep emotions are highly magnetic. When we find ourselves hitting rock bottom, it is then that we are creating desire for something more than what we have currently experienced in our lives. These incredibly powerful emotions are tremendous magnets. Although we often fail to realize the potential in the emotions of despair, within them lies hidden power. When we are in the throes of desperation, we are unconsciously begging the universe for something more.

Why Enabling Never Works

Many of us are guilty of enabling others, as well as trying to manipulate others into enabling us. And although most of us have realized that enabling never helps others get well, nor does it ever serve us, how many of us truly understand why this is so on a quantum level?

The world is an energetic place. It is a place that is governed by vibrations, waves, and magnetism. Emotions have the ability to charge the energetic totality of a being with particular energetic charges. When we are happy and upbeat, we *feel* positive. When we are downtrodden and hopeless, we *feel* negative.

We often hear people saying that birds of a feather tend to flock together, and if we applied this understanding to a family or a couple in relation to their energetic set points, we might say something like, "Those people were made for each other. They are all so negative. They all think and behave the same way."

People generally tend to befriend, marry, and share conflict with others who share similar vibes to their own.

Owning Our Stuff

The information you are receiving in this book has one main purpose, and that purpose is to help you fan the flames of Self-responsibility. When you are finally ready to deliberately and consciously refuse to ever see yourself as a victim again, your life begins to shift. It is not that we cannot do a thing. It is that we do not challenge the thinking that created the idea that we were incapable of doing what we wish that is holding us back.

This book is meant to challenge every thought you currently hold about Self, the world, and others in it. It is meant to shove you off the couch that has become the comfort zone in your mind. It has been written with tough love, a guiding hand, and an empathetic ear. It has been written from the aspect of my mind that confidently resides in a state of knowing. I write from a place in my consciousness that has me believing I am connected to everything, and everything is connected to me. I have learned to own that all I experience in the outer world is but a reflection of some aspect of my inner world that represents the relationship my inner divine Self-experiences with the aspect of Self *others* helped create. My journey has been to master my own perceptions and to come into alignment with who I was born to be, and to successfully soothe any complicated illusions anyone in my outer world ever imprinted into my subconscious mind.

I understand I am no longer a victim, and that only when I posture myself as such do I experience suffering. However, it was of the utmost importance while on my healing journey that I got in touch with and tapped into the child victim I once was. Seeing her, feeling her, and hearing her, the powerless little girl I once was allowed me to open the heavy door that held behind it all the feelings I was once thought I had no right to own. Although the moments I stood in front of that door and experienced the tsunami of emotions that rifled through it and through me were some of the most excruciating moments of my life, the relief that always arrived once the emotions filtered through was beautifully blissful and calming.

Patience, Dear One

So many of us who are wounded have been searching so long that we often feel frustrated when we think about how long it has taken us to get emotionally sober. I caution you in this area. I have learned that patience is a necessary component to true emotional recovery. It took years to impress your mind with false illusions of Self, and it will take some time for you to unravel those illusions, to process the feelings you were taught to deny, to allow yourself to experience them, and to begin laying down new tracks of belief systems in your mind before you are able to begin molding your life in a more deliberate fashion. But, Dear Ones, it will happen. You will be healed.

Challenges and Strategy Steps

1. Enmeshment

Enmeshment is a dysfunctional way of relating to others. When we are enmeshed with someone, our moods are impacted by the moods of the other. If the person we are enmeshed with is up, then so are we. If the person we are enmeshed with is down, so too do we become.

Enmeshing can also be a relating *style*. Many ACoAs and adults from dysfunctional families have so few boundaries that often we do not know how NOT to enmesh with those around us. It is quite often that we enmesh with *everything* around us. We enmesh with our emotions, other people's emotions, our moods, other people's moods, how other people think, and what other people do.

Being enmeshed implies we fail to understand the concept of boundaries in an array of situations.

Varying and Possible Causes of Enmeshment

- Unclear, permeable, inconsistent family boundary systems
- Improper and insufficient bonding between child and parents
- Shaming the child when independency is attempted
- Programming the child to fear the world and others
- Inconsistent family rules and norms

- Terrorizing family experiences that happen consistently and unpredictably
- Treating the child with indifference

There are a plethora of causative experiences that create enmeshment, but the primary agent seems to be a disregard for individual psychological, physical, emotional, and spiritual boundaries within families.

The Effects of Enmeshment

Enmeshment is a learned pattern of relating. When children are hovered over and/or continually raked over the coals emotionally, they are taught that they have no right to think, feel, or behave of their own accord. Instead they are brainwashed to believe that others must approve of what they do, think, and feel. Hovering over a child deprives the child of individual exploration, and undermines the child's instinct to try to think, feel, and do on his/her own.

- Unclear boundaries cause us to improperly believe we need to cling to others for emotional, psychological, or physical survival.
- Improper and insufficient bonding creates attachment needs to others that are rooted in insecurity. Because the bond between mother/father and child is incomplete, the child has been denied the chance to grow his/her emotional legs. This psychological unsteadiness creates a feeling of unworthiness in the Being, becoming the cornerstone for all future born insecurities about Self, which only feeds the unconscious need to enmesh with rather than relate as an individual to others.
- Shaming the child when he/she attempts to think unlike the rest of the family creates tremendous fear of having love and

attention withdrawn, which enhances the unconscious need to attach to others, and to please them. Fear of displeasing others enhances the child's insecurities while at same time reinforces his/her need to enmesh and cling.

- Programming a child to fear the world undermines a child's natural intuition to challenge and conquer new experiences. Brainwashing the child to believe that the world is a terrible place diminishes his/her desire to individuate, and amplifies the unconscious need to enmesh, cling, and attach to others.

- Inconsistent family rules and norms infuse the child with the sense that life is a disordered process, and that nothing is safe or stable. Because the need for security and safety is innate, children will learn to cling to the nearest person to them in search of that security and safety. As adults many of us deny red flags because we fear being alone so terribly, because we have been brainwashed and undermined as children.

- Terrorizing family experiences cause us to want to cling to others for that much needed sense of safety and security. We will cling to whomever is in our life at the time, in search of feeling safe. Because we have not been taught to honor Self, we do not naturally look within for the safety and security we need.

- When we are treated with indifference as children, we are brainwashed in big and in small ways to believe we are unworthy. This feeling of unworthiness creates great anxiety. This anxiety causes us to fear being alone, and increases our unconscious need to finally feel seen, valid, and worthy. It won't matter to us if our partners are abusers, liars, or cheats. It will only matter that there is a body in the water to cling to.

Strategy Step to Help Heal Enmeshment
The Rubber Band Visualization Tool

Goal:

These strategies are designed to help YOU recognize and learn HOW TO detangle your emotions and thoughts from others.

Part One:

- Imagine that you and everyone you know are one giant ball of thick rubber bands. See yourself somewhere layered in the middle, and imagine that all the people you know are clinging to you much like the rubber bands in a ball layer themselves tightly on top of one another.
- Once you have that visual in your mind, I want you to understand that the rubber bands represent individual thoughts and that your job is to separate your thoughts from that ball of confusion.
- Imagine taking one rubber band off at a time and then placing them one by one on a table in front of you.
- Notice the space between each rubber band.
- Keep separating those rubber bands and placing them down in front of you one by one.
- Understand that every rubber band you separate and detach from the bunch represents an individual's right to think, feel, and behave in a way that is of their right and of their choosing.
- After removing about twenty or so rubber bands, I want you to imagine that the next rubber band you remove represents you—mind, body, and soul.
- Place the rubber band on the table in front of you.
- Notice the space between you and all the other rubber bands.

- Feel the independence of that rubber band.
- Feel what it feels like to be no longer enmeshed with the other rubber bands.

Part Two:

- Take out your journal and begin writing about how you think the rubber band might feel now that it has detached from the pack. Include all the emotions you identify. Do not censor what comes up for you. ALL emotions are valid and are trying to show you something deeper.

For instance, a Rubber Band Journaling Exercise might sound like this:

"Today while practicing my Rubber Band Visualization exercise I noticed that at first I felt quite excited, happy, and free. But as I kept visualizing removing more rubber bands from the ball, I began to feel afraid. I think the fearful feeling was showing me that I do not know any other way of relating, and so I suppose it is the fear of the unknown. I suppose one of the reasons I stay enmeshed is because I fear taking care of myself, or for taking total responsibility for myself. Also, if I detach fully, then I won't be able to manipulate others into taking care of me. Detachment means I am totally responsible for my happiness as well as my unhappiness, and as exhilarating as that is, I must learn to accept that it is normal to feel afraid about trying to live emotionally free of other's opinions. I can accept the anxiety right now because I know that is normal. I also know that if I keep going, I will succeed and begin attracting really healthy others into my life. I can focus on that feeling, while at same time allow and be nurturing to the part of me that is a bit anxious about the unknowns I have yet to make my new friends."

AIMS ACHIEVED BY INCORPORATING ENMESHMENT HEALING STRATEGY

It is important to keep in mind that enmeshment is about non-choice. When one is enmeshed, he/she is a feather in the wind. He/she reacts to others moods, ideas, choices, wants, and actions. The concept of choice is nonexistent, which is why it is so crucial to flex our *choice* muscles—the muscles in our minds that allow us to think on our own two feet without needing to be approved of by others.

The Rubber Band and Slow Motion Thought Therapy exercises are created to help you begin understanding the idea of differentiation and individuality. You are different from anyone you know, as no one else on this planet has had your exact, unique experiences. And that's awesome, because it makes you. Not only that, but when you face the reality that it is virtually impossible to find someone who processes information and experiences precisely as you do, you begin to also understand that you could never precisely understand someone else's perceptions either. There is a great sense of liberation that arrives when we begin honoring ourselves as well as others for the unique individuals we all truly are.

2. Childlike Responses

Adult children of alcoholics (ACoAs), as well as any adult child from any dysfunctional home, can be likened to war veterans. Just like the sound of a gunshot might elicit a posttraumatic stress-related emotional response in a war veteran, children caught in battles at homes have deeply rooted triggers to trauma. Many of us used disassociation as a way to escape the fear, anxiety, loneliness, pain, abuse, and isolation. By zoning out and taking our minds somewhere else, we were able to release some of the pressure we were feeling internally when we were innocent and dependent on the beings abusing us.

To escape the pain of being taunted as a child by family members as well as peers, I would "float away." I found various ways to help me escape the pain of not feeling wanted, needed, or loved. When being chastised, ridiculed, labeled, and pushed away, I would pull individual strands of hair out of my head. The entire process of selecting just the right hair, twirling it around my finger, anticipating the slightest tug on my scalp, was ritualistic and in my opinion life-saving.

When innocent children suffer emotional trauma, many factors come into play. The brain's first order of business is survival, not emotional development. When an innocent child is raised in a home that is unpredictable, full of chaos, rage, screaming, yelling, beatings, addiction, indifference, and the like, it is all but impossible not to get stuck in early stages of emotional development. Because our brains' prioritizing our utmost need to survive stunted our normal emotional development processes, as adults many of us are void of proper coping skills. Today we react to situations much like the younger children we once were.

Some of our childlike responses include:

- We fear authority and authority-type figures.
- We whine when we don't get our way.
- We manipulate others into doing the things we want them to do.
- We guilt others for not supporting our every idea.

- We stomp our feet, throw things, curse, yell, and scream when we do not feel listened to.
- We blame others for why we are sad, lonely, frustrated, angry, and stuck in our lives.
- We allow others to take advantage of us.
- We take advantage of others.
- We stay stuck in places that don't feel right—still thinking like a once helpless little child without choices.
- We fear getting other people angry.
- We avoid confrontation.
- We do not speak up for ourselves.
- We override other people's opinions.
- We do not respect other people's opinions.
- We do not respect our own opinions.
- We seek validation just as we did when we were small.
- We don't tell the truth.
- We lie by omission.
- We steal for no reason.
- We really believe we are powerless just like when we were small.
- We feel stuck and react rather than take rational inventories of what is really going on in our lives.
- We over idealize sweet talkers.
- We fall for words rather than deeds.

It is important to note that there are valid and logical biological reasons for why we ACoAs think and behave like children when we feel threatened in any way. The brain is wired primarily to help us survive. The survival instinct is found in the almond-shaped bunch of neurons called the amygdala located in our temporal lobe. Also located in the temporal lobe is the hippocampus. If any of us are stuck in loops of reactivity that remind of us of how we behaved when we were six years old, we can thank our well-intended amygdala and hippocampus.

I remember being fascinated back in nursing school by all the distinct functions of the brain. Insatiably curious, I have never stopped researching how the brain functions and discovering ways in which I could help myself understand exactly what I needed to do in order to change any behavior, belief, or patterns that were rolling around in my mind. While studying psychology allowed me to understand what I needed (what all children needed) in order to mature and live life as a well-adjusted adult someday, learning the ins and outs about the brain validated whatever I hypothesized about what milestones I needed to hit in order to master myself psychologically.

Strategy Step
The Eye In The Sky

Goal:

The aim of this exercise is to help you begin perceiving yourself as the true authority over your life, rather than as a powerless child stuck in old, dysfunctional patterns of thought that no longer serve you. As you learn to master this exercise, you will soon begin reaping limitless rewards.

For this exercise you will need:

- Quiet, sacred space
- Fifteen minutes
- Journal
- Pen

In order to interrupt the loops in our mind, we are going to need to give the brain new information. The hippocampus is closely related to the amygdala in our brain and is also located in the temporal lobe. The hippocampus is responsible for creating new memories, but has a really tough time doing so when the stress-related glucocorticoids are floating around in our bloodstream. Glucocorticoids hinder the brain's ability to create new memories, so becoming of calm mind must be the primary priority.

As children we were programmed to feel powerless, and eventually many of us gave up believing we could ever escape our loneliness, powerlessness, bad luck, and anxiety. This patterned behavior of thought is called "learned helplessness." Because we were victims and powerless once, unfortunately many of us have accepted that as our fate.

Just as it is nearly impossible for a child to learn new things when he/she is powerless and forced to live in survival, adults also struggle with learning new information, as our survival patterns are still going strong. Although we are no longer six, seven, or eight, many of us still live our lives as if we are powerless children.

Because we were never taught to question our realities, today we live in denial of our true personal power. It is possible to create new memories in the hippocampus, and our ability to do so has been with us all the time. Being raised by aloof, self-absorbed, disconnected others has conditioned us to seek validation outside of Self rather than to rely on the power of the Self that was within us all the while. There is an absolute divine order to this universe as well as to our lives, but searching for those truths is a matter of an individual's free will and choice.

Take five deep breaths, and imagine yourself ascending into the clouds. Imagine seeing yourself sitting comfortably on a large, cozy white cloud. Imagine looking down at yourself right now in your sacred space.

For this exercise you are going to visualize yourself looking down upon your life like you might look down onto a stage that holds the characters in your life.

Once you have achieved this visualization of sitting on a cloud in the sky, read these key reprogramming phrases aloud.

- I am not six years old anymore.
- No one is the boss over me.
- I can make decisions that are in my best interest.
- I can trust my internal guidance.
- I know my Self is leading the way.
- I know I do not need other's validation.
- I know I must seek my own validation.
- I know I can trust what makes me happy.
- I know I can walk away from those who drain me.
- I know it is better to be alone than to be abused.
- I know that all love must start with Self-love.
- I know I am worthy at my core.
- I know that the only thing wrong with me is what I have been programmed to think, feel, and believe about me.
- I know that I can think like an adult.
- I know I can take responsibility for how I feel, what I do, how much money I make, spend, and save.
- I know that happiness is rooted in acting up ideas of Self-love.
- I know that people who hurt me don't understand real love.
- I know I deserve people in my life who do understand real love.
- I know it is not my job to deny myself to make others happy.

AIMS ACHIEVED BY INCORPORATING ENMESHMENT HEALING STRATEGY

Mastering this exercise will infuse you with a true sense of personal power, esteem, strength, courage, and resolve. You will begin communicating with others on equal playing fields and will no longer knee-jerk react to other's whims, words, and behaviors.

Because so many adult children from emotionally neglectful homes are disengaged from their authentic self, many of the responses we give others are knee-jerk and reactionary at best. We do not respond from calm, centered places within our minds, and so we react rather than take the time to process the information being presented.

The above exercise helps to slow the mind down. It also helps the mind begin to feel less attached to outcomes, and what we think other people think we should say or do.

Adult children so often feel like marionettes on strings. And in many ways, until we begin to tap into our godlike Self, we are puppets. The strings others pull are tied to our programmed and patterned responses; the ones we learned in childhood.

Successful practices of the above exercise help your mind reframe how it perceives *you*, the being doing the pondering. Outside our deliberate and conscious decision-making mind, we are reactionary beings unaware there is a much healthier way of relating to others. Practicing this technique will allow you to respond to others in ways like:

- "I am not sure how I feel about that. Let me get back to you later after I have given it some thought and weighed out all my options."
- "I can see we are not going to agree on this right now, so let's step away and give this situation some more thought."
- "You and I have differing opinions, and that is quite all right. We simply do not see eye to eye on this, and that is fine. I can accept that you do not agree with me, and I also respect your

perspective. We can agree to disagree on this matter."

- "I really prefer to stay home tonight. But thank you for the invite. I appreciate it, but would like some 'me' time this evening."
- "No, I am sorry. I am unavailable to watch your dog that weekend. I know you will find someone who is totally available, which will help you feel more at ease."
- "No, I am sorry. That just does not feel quite right in my gut. I understand you do not understand my position, and that is fine. I understand how I feel, and I must go with that."
- "I must be totally honest with you. This relationship is not working out for me. I am hoping you find someone who is more suited for you. My feelings just are not into this relationship as much as I need them to be. I am sorry, but I am going to have to end this relationship with you. I wish you all the luck in the world finding someone who can appreciate you for you."

Learning how to not knee-jerk is an absolute must for wounded adult children. The simple although elusive ingredient, however, is personal truth. Adult children often find themselves lying when they do not have to. Because we have been conditioned to fear what others think and to deny how we feel, these two standpoints become toxic tonics that diminish our ability to connect to our divine Self.

Calming the mind requires discipline, but will help you discover the whispers of your individual soul.

3. Seek Validation For The Self—Outside Of Self

Abused adult children from dysfunctional homes tend to seek validation from others rather than seek to self-validate. Dysfunctional parents who are not connected to their own self are not self-aware. This lack of self-awareness in parents makes it impossible for them to comprehend the importance of validating their children's selves in an authentic, consistent manner.

I would dare to argue, however carefully, that I am of the belief that unaware parents are abusive, although unintentionally. When a parent denies their child nutrition, it is clear that abuse is taking place. In my mind there is little difference between a parent who starves a child nutritionally and a parent who starves a child psychologically. A child of eight or nine months could and probably would crawl to food left on a table to satisfy their physical hunger. It would be common sense for the child to do so, and the child would if he or she could get to the food, feed the body the nutrition it needed.

However, a child does not know it has a Self that needs to be fed somehow. A child does not know it is essential to feel *seen* on a psychological level in order to be able to grow emotionally and spiritually. A child does not understand that the feelings of abandonment, rejection, and the like are its soul's hunger pains. It is not as intrinsic to feed one's own Self as it is to feed one's hungry belly. If a child has had their hunger pains alleviated by the act of being fed, then a positive feedback system has been created, and therefore the child would have some program imprinted in their mind that has taught them how to alleviate hunger pains. Therefore, it must be presumed that if a child's emotional woes go unnoticed by unaware parents, the child's mind will be void of programming necessary to satisfy the emotional hunger.

Adults from dysfunctional homes who have no programming for how to feed the Self are disconnected from the Self. Because their emotions were ignored, ridiculed, chastised, or treated with indifference, their perception of Self is muted, garbled, or misunderstood. The Self is an aspect of our conscious perception of the being that is **us** that must be turned on—or actualized. Unlike the ability to breathe, it is not a given.

When a child is born, the umbilical cord is severed from the mother. At this point a healthy child's lungs begin to draw in oxygen from the environment, which takes over the duty of respiration. In a healthy child all the proper roadways of capillaries, neurons, and synapses are in clear working order. There are no bumps in the road, and breathing independently happens quite naturally. Unlike the roadways that allow breathing to happen spontaneously, the act of connecting to Self is not spontaneous. The art of loving and acknowledging the Self can be, and should be, a lifelong journey that is hallmarked by experiences one lives, and by the lessons those experiences teach. However, how can the journey of Self be had if one has been denied the necessary introduction to Self? It is the role of mother and of father to introduce the child to his/her Self through consistent, positive, age-appropriate reinforcement. Offering the child age-appropriate choices, as well as specifically telling a child that he/she is good, good enough, and capable of anything he/she desires, helps the child become comfortably acquainted with the concept of a good, worthy Self.

To deepen the issue for a child who has been born to parents who are unaware they are unaware, because no commitment is being made to connect to the child's Self from the parent's authentic Self, the child never knows that security, peace, and love have been locked within them all the while. Because they have not been conditioned to tune into Self, they spend their lives ignorant and tuned away from Self instead. The plot only thickens as abused adult children age chronologically. Stuck in immature patterns of fight or flight, reinforced by hypervigilant perceptions of the world, adult children are unaware that they are stuck in loops. They are also unaware that oftentimes they/we seek validation, to the point of obsession, from others in an unconscious attempt to acquire some food for our Self's soul. Being validated from the outside is one of the first orders of business for a new soul, and because that need has not been met due to improper psychological parenting, the being continues to seek the required validation from outside of Self for the rest of his/her natural life.

To add corn starch to the thickened emotional plot that can be a wounded adult child's internal and external world is the idea that on a quantum level a being can only attract that which the child understands is love. As adults many of us attract similar energy beings to one or both of our parents, unaware we are drawing to us the energetic equivalent of our own unique vibrational/emotional set point. Many of us go through life recycling, repeating, and recreating the same empty and unfulfilling experiences we endured in childhood, completely blind to the fact that we are simply still thinking like children, stuck in the patterns etched in our temporal lobes.

Some Of The Ways We Seek Validation Outside Of Self

- We enable others instead of holding them accountable, fearing we might make them angry and cause them to walk away, triggering our fear of abandonment.
- We anticipate the needs of others, secretly wishing to cause others to depend on us in unhealthy ways so that they never leave us, helping us to try to control ever possibly facing abandonment.
- We say yes when we mean no, and no when we mean yes because we fear making others angry, and possibly causing them to leave us, helping us to try to control ever possibly facing abandonment.
- We tolerate being ignored, abused, lied to, chastised, and the like so that we do not have to enforce a boundary, and possibly have to face abandonment and loss.
- We seek ways in which we can become subservient to others, secretly hoping we might be able to convince others we are

worthy to keep around.

- We do not ask for what we need, want, or desire because we fear being seen as selfish, and sometimes because we want others to perceive us as need-less. Coming off as need-less, in our minds, makes us feel like others will be more willing to keep us around if we don't ask for too much.
- We deny our own pain for the sake of keeping others content.
- We deny our own needs, in spite of how others ignore ours and expect us to honor theirs.
- We focus completely on the needs of others, only reinforcing our alienation from Self.

The main problem that must be resolved is the initial energy leak created in our beings when we were first born and seeking to complete our energetic infinity bond with primarily mother, but also father.

It is essential for a child's emotional well-being that he/she feel bonded or connected especially to mother, but also to father. When we are born to parents who are not connected to their own divine Self, it is all but impossible for mother to be able to connect authentically to her newborn. Unresolved emotional issues in mother will prevent the most authentic bonds from being created. Neurotic, enmeshment bonds are not healthy, authentic bonds. Enmeshment is not authentic as it suggests that the parents are leeching energy in some way from their innocent child in an attempt to feel seen/worthy/valid themselves.

In this strategy step we will be attempting to mother our own selves, and in so doing teach and program ourselves to seek our own validation rather than to continue to seek validation from outside of Self and risk attracting unaware similar energy beings to our parents into our experiences of today.

Strategy Step
Integrating Mind, Body, and Soul

Goal:

The goal of this exercise is to connect the three divine aspects of Self—mind, body, and soul. By seeking innumerable ways to validate the emotional cues of spirit, we learn to allow from the mind space, honor the spiritual space, and act upon that which we feel, need, want, and desire through the vehicle that is our physical body.

Learning to allow our spirits to be heard affords us the opportunity to become integrated—mind, body, and soul. In this exercise we learn to do what our mothers and fathers did not do; honor our emotions, needs, wants, and desires. When we learn to act upon our emotions, needs, wants, and desires, we encourage the much needed neurological growth of necessary pathways of neurons that help us connect to all perceptions of us that represent the sum of who we are as unique beings.

In healthy child-parent relationships, love is exchanged easily from child to parent and from parent to child. But when a child is born to an emotionally unavailable parent, the energy exchange between the two is not as healthy as it could be. It is not one of pure positive love. Instead the energy exchanged is negatively charged. The child absorbs the energies of others, as he or she is sponge-like and has no emotional defenses against the energies in the home. Emotions like anxiety, depression, guilt, and shame are compounded by the child's innate need to feel seen and validated on the soul level by beings who are in denial about their own feelings, let alone as to what their true role is as parent to the child.

This seemingly simple exercise will help you connect to your godlike Self. It will help you foster your conscious understanding of Self, as well as help teach you how to pay closer attention to your personal emotional cues from spirit.

For this exercise you will need:

- Journal
- Index cards
- Pen
- Fifteen minutes in the morning
- Quiet, sacred space

Part One:

Seek The Frozen Emotions

- In your journal please draw two circles approximately three inches in diameter with one inch of space between them.
- Label the first circle with the name of the person who you believe most negatively impacted the way you see yourself today. To help you identify the person whose name you will associate with this circle, you may ask yourself the questions below.
- Label the second circle with your name.

Ask yourself:

- Who in my life made me perceive my Self as unworthy?
- Who did I love who I felt rejected me?
- Who made me feel like I was unworthy to be loved back?
- Who was I trying to gain validation from, but rarely received it?
- Who made me feel invisible?
- Who made me feel the most ashamed?
- Who do I believe enjoyed making me feel uncomfortable?

(You may have to draw a number of these diagrams to represent more than one impressionable relationship you experienced as a child, while you were formulating ideas about your self-worth, before you can truly uncover all your emotional energy leaks.)

Please do not concern yourself with how many diagrams you will need to draw. The goal is to uncover the hiccups in your memory banks, and to resolve old patterns of negative thought processes and beliefs that keep you stuck and repeating the experiences you wish to cease recreating.

- In the space between the two circles, write down as many of the emotions you recall feeling or sensing as a child when you were experiencing the other person in your life.

Some of the emotions you may have experienced might include:

- Abandoned
- Rejected
- Not good enough
- Unworthy
- Bad
- Selfish
- Incompetent
- Stupid
- Ugly
- Evil
- Wrong
- Empty
- Sad
- Lonely
- Angry

- Frustrated
- Disillusioned
- Self-pity
- Despair
- Depressed
- Anxious
- Unease
- Foggy
- Detached
- Afraid
- Terrified
- Hopeless
- Powerless
- Rage
- Heavy
- Exhausted
- Drained
- Paranoid
- Invisible

Part Two:

Allow Yourself To Feel The Frozen Emotions

Many emotions that surface within us, we experience as kinks in our energetic bodies. Our bodies are electrical circuits. Emotions determine what charges are being carried in our electrical field. When we fear and experience guilt and shame over any emotion, our bodies are impacted negatively in innumerable ways.

Humans are intended to feel their feelings, just as nerve endings are intended to feel pain and sense temperatures. Feeling is key to survival.

Emotions are like water. They are supposed to keep flowing. Emotions are meant to flow like water through cheesecloth, and when they are pushed down instead, much like stagnant water that has been prevented from free flowing, we begin to rot from the inside out.

In this part of the exercise, you are going to learn how to feel and allow all the emotions that you pushed down inside of you when you were a powerless child.

- Label an index card with each emotion you have identified.
- After writing out your flash cards, spend a few minutes looking at each card, and try to connect to the emotion.
- Spend fifteen minutes a day trying to imagine what the particular emotion felt like when you were in the moments experiencing them.
- Note any images, words, or phrases that come up in your journal.

For instance:

Powerless: "*I remember feeling powerless whenever Daddy started slamming his fist against the kitchen table. I remember feeling afraid, terrified, and the knot in my stomach that would show up every time I noticed Daddy getting upset. I remember the way his face would get all twisted, and how tense his body would seem. I remember Mom's facial expressions changing and watching concern sweep over her face. I remember feeling frozen and like any moment the house was going to explode. I was about seven years old at the time.*"

- Once you have identified an emotion and you have been able to make a connection to some moment in time that gave birth to that emotion, allow the feelings and the memories to surface.

- Spend a few minutes honoring the experience of your inner child.
- Cry if that is what shows up for you, as crying is the way a soul takes a bath.
- Allow yourself approximately fifteen minutes each morning to SEEK and ALLOW your emotional blocks to surface.

Part Three:

Rewriting The Script

The third part of this process is designed to help you learn how to properly parent your own inner child.

Healthy parents know that it is crucial to their child's emotional development to learn how to allow whatever they feel to surface in appropriate ways. If a child is angry, it is best to acknowledge the child's right to feel angry, and to also help model for the child an appropriate way to deal with the feeling of anger.

Once you have filtered through your emotional flash cards, ask yourself this question:

- *How would I have liked my parents to address my emotions so that I would have learned how to feel, accept, process, and deal with them?*

- **Please write the answers you receive in your journal.**

Some examples of how you might answer this question:

Afraid. "*I wish my mom would have asked me why I was afraid. I wish she would have explained to me that Daddy had a difficult time controlling his anger and that his anger was not my fault. I wish my mom would have protected me from my dad and said something like, 'Frank, you're frightening the children. Please get a hold of yourself. We can discuss what is bothering you later when the children are in bed. It's our job to make them feel safe, Frank, not to fill them with fear.'*

"*I would have felt nurtured, safe, protected, validated, understood, seen, and worthy. If my mom had reacted that way to my honesty, I would have also learned that telling the truth was a good thing, and nothing to fear. If my mom had spoken like that to my dad, I would have also learned that I was important, and that boundaries are appropriate.*

"*If my dad had agreed with my mom, I would have learned so much from just that situation. I would have learned how to take constructive criticism, how to control my responses, how to hold myself accountable, and how to say 'I am sorry.'*"

NOTE: ALL EMOTIONS ARE VALID, ALTHOUGH RESPONSES TO OUR EMOTIONS ARE WHAT WE NEED TO MONITOR. IT IS CRUCIAL WE LEARN HOW <u>NOT TO</u> FEAR WHAT WE FEEL—AND INSTEAD LEARN TO EMBRACE WHAT WE FEEL AND FOCUS MORE ON THE BEHAVIOR THAT FOLLOWS AN EMOTION WE EXPERIENCE.

By teaching yourself healthier and more appropriate responses to old blocked emotions, your mind is offered new data to experiment with. During the course of the day, learn to allow what you feel to surface and then filter the emotion through this 1-2-3 process:

1. Accept the emotion you are experiencing.

2. Trust that the emotion is trying to tell you something.

3. Decide what you want to do about the emotion from a higher state of consciousness as opposed to falling back into old patterns of knee-jerk reactivity.

E-motion = energy in motion

To master our emotions, we must first learn to appreciate the fact that our emotions were designed to

stay in motion.

They were NOT designed to

become blocked, ignored,

or denied.

This does not imply that we are supposed to REACT to every emotion we experience in the physical world.

Instead, emotions are intended to flow through our beings like water in streams.

Our goal is to use our emotions as guides, not as a means to any end.

AIMS ACHIEVED BY INCORPORATING
HEALING INTEGRATION STRATEGY

Successfully learning how to uncover all the emotions we have been taught we had no right to feel and experience not only helps us unblock ourselves energetically, but it also allows us to learn how to feel our emotions and deal with them, rather than always trying to control them.

In addition, this process of seeking, allowing, feeling, and dealing helps us to stop seeking validation from outside of self. Through diligent practice of this emotional exercise, we learn to honor the blessing it is to seek within Self for guidance, rather than from others on the outside. Because we are learning to release shame, guilt, fear and self-doubt, we no longer need to seek validation from others as a way to mask our feelings of unworthiness. We are successfully learning how to honor the Self, and in so doing, we no longer neurotically feel the need to have others help us hide from shame. The shame begins to disappear along with the need to seek validation from outside of Self.

As we continue seeking old blocked energies, while at same time giving ourselves permission to finally experience these energies, we are learning to banish the shame associated with our emotions. Many of us are ashamed of any emotion we feel, and have been conditioned to stay stuck in patterns of fear and shame as opposed to learning how to allow our emotions to guide us along our life's path. This adversarial relationship, brainwashed into our belief systems, begins to fade as we learn to no longer fear our emotions.

4. Not Self-Actualized

One of the most noted characteristics of people who are self-actualized is their attention to solutions, rather than attention to problems. In a nutshell, one who is self-actualized has learned to tune into and act upon the guidance of self. Self-actualization is a process that represents personal growth. One who is self-actualized seeks growth and expansion of the self. It is the norm to wish to act upon a desire to learn something new and to master it. There is a sense of emotional forward moving momentum, opposed to emotional stagnation. Self-actualized beings tend to see their lives as opportunities to discover more about themselves, and about their world. Their glass is always half full, and when tragedy does occur their focus is set upon rising above what has occurred, rather than focusing on what has occurred without the desire or resolve to overcome.

Adult children from dysfunctional homes have a difficult time becoming self-actualized for a plethora of reasons.

- When a child is powerless and forced to live in states of fight or flight, the priority is survival, not personal self-development.
- When children are routinely criticized, their ability to honor the impulses and cues of Self are severely hindered.
- When children are judged by their parents, caretakers, siblings, and the like, their attention is focused on deflecting the next attack, not on honoring the cues of their soul.
- When children are not mirrored back a healthy sense of Self, they do not know they have a self and instead are alienated from the Self.
- When non self-actualized parents raise children, the children are denied the modeling for becoming self-actualized.
- When children are raised by beings who are problem-oriented rather than solution-oriented, the children are denied the coping skills necessary to become more self-actualized.

While there are adult children from dysfunctional homes who do in fact learn to become self-actualized, the majority of us struggle with feeling alien in our own skin. In addition to being denied healthy mirroring of self, which would have helped us to initiate some initial sense of self, many of us continued to be raised by others who failed to connect with us authentically throughout our lives. Because family members who were clueless to their own Self may have raised us, it was the dysfunctional norm for all to exist in zombielike states, detached from their authentic Selves.

Personal Story

I can recall being seven years old and wondering if I were real at all. I did not know where this sense of alienation was coming from, as I was just a small child. I do remember being extremely aware that I did not feel seen on a psychological level.

One afternoon I remember leaning in close to my mother's bedroom mirror. My eyes were green, but because no one in my family ever mentioned their color, and because my mother had routinely mentioned that my sister's eyes were blue like hers and my brother's eyes were brown like my father's, I wondered if perhaps I did not perceive colors like the rest of my family. I did not know how to ask, "Why is that you never mention the color of my eyes, yet you acknowledge the color of my sister and brother's eyes?" Instead, I internalized the feeling of non-acknowledgment.

As a child it was the dysfunctional norm to hide my feelings. Feelings were an inconvenient and dirty little problem. They made for bumps in the road and overturned apple carts, which was akin to murder or robbery. We dared not express our anger, sadness, or disappointment in our home as children. We understood it was our job to detach and pretend we were okay even when we weren't.

Many years later, I understand as well as appreciate how and why it was not possible for me to become self-actualized until I embarked on my recovery process. I was conditioned to detach from the essence of me, my divine self, for the sake of other's need to stay in complete control. As a non-self-actualized adult, I embarked on a life unaware I was leaking energy, and on an unconscious level had a severe need to somehow feel validated externally.

Now I understand why I always felt like a phony. Now I understand that because I was programmed to deny my Self, I did. Now I understand that feeling powerless to be able to express my true emotions as a child, I instead learned to detach from my inner Self—for the sake of my parents' approval and my emotional safety. I also understand that the survival skills I learned as a child became ingrained in my brain as a way to help me survive my circumstances. And now I understand I no longer need those old patterns, because I am no longer that powerless little girl who needs to pretend for the sake of seeking other's approval.

Lisa A. Romano
ACoA Dry Home Survivor
Life Coach/Author

Strategy Step
Let's Get Cognitive

Goal:

The goal of this exercise is to help you with nurturing the connection between your conscious mind and your authentic true self objectively as opposed to reactively.

The conscious mind reacts to the emotions
that seep through the veil
that separates the conscious mind
from the subconscious mind.
What then, if what is in the subconscious mind
is dysfunctional and an illusion?
What then, if the subconscious mind
has been taught to deny and even hate the authentic Self?
Can a man claim he is thinking
if in fact he is but merely recycling what has been programmed into
his subconscious mind when he was powerless
as a child to challenge what was being programmed?
True thinking requires reason and logic.
Is it reasonable or logical to expect a being to be happy
if he has been taught to believe that at the essence, he is
unworthy, and when he has not been taught
to question the contents of his subconscious mind?
How then can a man who has been programmed to believe he is of
no worth ever hope to be of worth?
How then can a society expect those of that society who have been
programmed to believe themselves worthless
to find worth in themselves,
and thus be worthy members of a society, contributing willingly of
themselves for the better of that society?
How then can a man who has been brainwashed to believe in his
worthlessness
ever be expected to see worth in another man?
If the outer is a reflection of the inner
it is the inner that needs to shift.
When we change the way we perceive the Self,
the way we see others changes as well.
As it is below the veil,

so shall it be above the veil.
What has been sown
so shall man reap,
even if what has been sown
is not of man's own.

When the subconscious programming is deeply rooted in patterns that has one denying the innocence of Self, emotions like guilt and shame are the end results. A delicate crystal-like web becomes the mind as one becomes fragile in their being. Silent emotional terror becomes the norm as the brainwashed victim becomes paralyzed by fear. This unchallenged mind has been taught to disown the voice of Self rather than to create his/her reality in alignment with the authentic, innate Self.

To heal, one needs to learn how to objectify his/her thought process while at the same time learns to hear or tap into the faint whispers of the immortal Self that never stops sending guidance. The aim of this exercise is to raise the volume of Self in spite of the crystal web we need to navigate. Much like the sight of an illumined lighthouse miles ahead on shore a skilled sea captain must keep his eye on as he steers his vessel through a storm, the faint voice of Self becomes the focus as opposed to the storm.

Below is an example of how one might utilize the power of deliberate cognition to turn up the volume of Self.

Let's say you are driving down the street, and you notice a dance studio to your left. The banner in the window reads, "Free Adult Dance Lesson Tonight at 7:00 p.m. All adults over the age of 40 are welcome!" and you immediately sense that you would really enjoy checking that out. In fact, you already know you are going to be free and that there is nothing holding you back from taking that dance class.

The moment you read the banner your heart quickens with excitement, but in the next moment you notice all the old programming begin to kick in. You notice voices in your head saying things like: *"Oh, you can't go there. Who do you think you are? Do you want to make a fool out of yourself? You can't dance. That's a joke. What will your mother and father say when you tell them YOU took a dance class for people who are over forty?"*

In a flash the cue from the authentic Self is lost amidst the rhetoric of the beliefs other people programmed into your mind (the crystal web of codependency created through subconscious programming: "I am not enough"). These fears aren't even yours, but because you have been conditioned to deny the cues of Self, you do.

Breaking Free of Old Patterns

The goal of these mental exercises is to help you learn to flex the cognitive and neurological connections to the belly of your own **Self**. In order to feel real, authentic, and truly alive, one must learn to hear the cues of one's own Self, and act upon them if personal growth is to be achieved.

The Self has one purpose, and that is to become actualized in the physical world. When you follow inner guidance, you are stepping into alignment with the same energies that create universes.

You will need:

- Notebook
- Pen
- Private time in a car, bus, subway, or in a public place

1. Whenever you are in your car or in public, you are to begin observing the workings of your mind. Your goal is to observe your thoughts much like you would clouds rolling by overhead on a windy day. Do not attach to the thoughts. Simply observe them.

2. Mentally note any cues you observe from your inner Self that might suggest trying something new, like a restaurant, or perhaps taking a different route home.

3. When you notice a new cue, mentally note it and then wait and listen for what kinds of thoughts or programs begin to follow. Simply observe the type of self-talk that appears once you notice a cue from the Self. Did you think about taking a jog after work? Was the self-talk that appeared after that positive cue negative or supportive? Did your self-talk support your innate desire to take a jog or did it negate it?

4. Note how you feel as you begin to desire to hear your own voice. Most beings are not aware that their minds have the ability to expand on command. You have the power to say, "Hey, wait a minute. I heard that desire to go for a jog, and now I am hearing the negative self-talk as well. I can see how my authentic Self is continually trying to get born, or actualized, and also how my subconscious programming prevents me from ever acting upon the guidance of my authentic Self. Today I am going to change my programming. I am actually going to go home and put a pair of running sneakers on, no matter what my old programming is rewinding in my mind. I am not my programming. The programming was **done** to me. I am more than what has been done to me."

AIMS ACHIEVED BY INCORPORATING
THE *LET'S GET COGNITIVE* STRATEGY

By deliberately choosing time to observe your mind's inner self-talk, you are learning to exercise the power of your consciousness. It is improbable to presume that one can go from a state of reactivity to a state of consistent deliberate contemplation and expect to maintain that higher state of awareness without slipping back into old patterns of thinking without first practicing higher mental states.

Many of us have spent our lives on autopilot, reacting to other's opinions as well as to our own dysfunctional programs. It can be quite the exhausting experience to shift. When we are shifting to higher states of consciousness, we feel drained. Shifting to higher states of consciousness often feels like we are stepping in front of speeding trains, and in many ways we are.

Setting aside specific times throughout our day to practice deliberate, conscious expansion helps us to get more acquainted with the power of our minds. We have spent many years reacting to programs and belief patterns that are rooted in the subconscious mind. It will take commitment, dedication, patience, and practice to learn to think above the veil.

5. Struggle With Guilt And Shame

Many adults who have been emotionally neglected and/or abused in childhood tend to suffer from guilt and shame. When a child is born to a being who does not, for whatever reason, have the capacity to bond with that child, he/she suffers in innumerable ways. At birth an invisible infinity energy loop is supposed to be established between mother and child. When this infinity bond is insufficient, the energy system of the newborn child is negatively impacted.

A newborn child is supposed to feel connected to his/her mother and father. This connection, although invisible, is a tangible band of positive love energy (bond) that is exchanged from the parent's heart center to the child's heart center. Because it is innate to gain a connection to mother and father, a child never stops seeking to **feel** *seen* by his/her parents, regardless of how often the parents may have abused, neglected, or abandoned the child.

If human beings were born with the ability to see energy exchanges between parents and their children, we would witness many energetic hemorrhages. Children enter this world primarily with one agenda, and that is to feel connected, valued, and loved by mother and father. When a child is born to an alcoholic, narcissist, or indifferent parent, attempts made by the child to connect to that parent are often met with resistance. In situations like these, children hemorrhage love energy. Perhaps even worse than the energetic hemorrhage is the idea that the parents are blind to their child's suffering.

The tribal instinct to bond is innate. It is unnatural to feel rejected or invisible to one's tribe. It is necessary for human survival to feel bonded to one's own tribe. If it were not for the ability to empathize with others, humans may have killed one another off long ago. Because human beings are designed to yawn after witnessing another human being yawn, we understand the innateness of feeling seen. It is unnatural to feel invisible, unwanted, rejected, abandoned, and unloved by one's own tribe. Every cell in a child's body is wired to feel a sense of belonging to one's own tribe. When this energetic/emotional/psychological (body, spirit, mind) milestone is unmet, the innocent being suffers a disconnect not only between his/her own tribe, but to the authentic Self as well.

Not feeling bonded/connected to mother and father infuses the child with ill assumptions about Self. In the galleys of the child's mind he/

she wonders, "Am I bad? Am I not good enough to be loved? I must be broken. Mommy can't see me. Daddy never hugs me. I must not be worthy. It is me that is wrong." When bonds are insufficient there is no balance in the relationships. The child is seeking love, and mother and father may be too blocked emotionally to even notice.

There is little doubt that the environment we adult children were raised in impacted our ability to relate to Self as well as to others in healthy ways. We were impressionable sponges, powerless to what data was being collected by our psyches.

Ways we manifest feeling rejected by our tribe, and thus disconnected from Self, include:

- Hypervigilance
- Distrusting
- Perfectionistic
- Super responsible
- Irresponsible
- Self-critical
- Neurotically sensitive
- Insensitive
- Obsessive
- Fear filled
- Anxious
- Doubtful
- Suffer from nightmares
- Have autoimmune disorders
- Doubt Self
- Caretaking
- Enabling
- Disassociating from our emotions

- Suffering from PTSD symptoms
- Codependency
- Clingy
- Manipulative
- In tugs of war with needing love and fearing love
- Struggling to figure out what healthy sex really is
- Lack personal and external boundaries
- Over reactive
- Depressed
- Confused
- Exhausted
- Empty
- Isolated
- Fear we are crazy

We adult children of the dysfunctional who have grown up feeling ignored fundamentally may recognize that we are not to blame for the way in which we process information. However, many of us struggle with feeling guilty and ashamed of how we feel, the way we think, and for how we react. In spite of knowing on an intellectual level much of how we feel is not our fault, we shroud ourselves with guilt and shame. Because we may have internalized the rejection of our tribe, we find it difficult to separate our perception of Self from the shame that feeling of being rejected created so long ago.

Periods of Sobriety

Inconsistent emotional connections also tend to reinforce our feelings of guilt and shame. If your alcoholic was nurturing when they were sober and rejected you when they were drunk, you learned it was unsafe to trust. In addition, many of us internalized the rejection and unconsciously assumed we were somehow responsible for the rejection.

Dry Homes

For those of us out there who did not have alcohol to point to, but lived with emotionally unstable parents who were unpredictable, we, too, have been wounded deeply. Because we were born to parents who were emotionally erratic, we were forced to sleep with one eye open. Every day was like another stint in a war zone. In addition, because our parents were in denial of their own illnesses, as well as about how deeply they were abusing us, today many of us are stuck in defensiveness. Our tiny minds were programmed not to trust, and so as adults, we struggle with letting our guard down, and with even trusting our own divine souls.

Abused Children Are Wired For Survival
Not Growth And Expansion

Adult children from dysfunctional homes have been emotionally derailed. Although we entered into this world with the ability to grow and expand, our childhoods have stunted our emotional growth. Many of us were forced to live with parents who were unpredictable, hostile, violent, and chaotic. Constantly needing to monitor our home environments for the next collapse patterned us to live in states of survival, and to very much feel stuck, or frozen. Unfortunately, we may still feel stuck today. Feeling stuck impedes our ability to grow and expand as individuals. Unlike children who were born to healthy, supporting caretakers, we have been raised in homes that were unsupportive of growth. Today it is not our norm to seek growth in our everyday lives. Instead, we seek to avoid pain rather than to seek pleasure. We needed to stay on guard as children because we understood we were powerless. Staying hypervigilant helped us survive. In order to grow and expand today, we will need to rewire our perception of Self as well as our circumstances. No longer are we six years old and powerless. We can think. We can choose. We can say no. We can say yes.

Strategy Step
Setting Achievable Goals

Goal:

Research has proven that in order to feel happy, human beings must be engaging in activities that allow for growth and expansion. To combat our guilt and shame, we will deliberately choose to set achievable goals that will not only help us honor our childhood experiences, but will also help us learn how to make ourselves happy. The aim of this exercise is to help us teach ourselves how to wire our brains in such a way that allows for us to seek growth and expansion of Self. This exercise helps us "see" our inner selves, and thus feel connected to Self. In this way we create a tribal bond with the divine Self, and integrate mind, body, and soul.

For this exercise you will need:

- Journal
- Pen
- Quiet time each morning (ten to fifteen minutes)

Objective:

Write two goal lists. One goal list includes five immediate goals for the day, and the other includes goals that you will complete by the end of your day.

For instance:

Immediate Goals For The Day

1. Brush teeth
2. Make bed
3. Take dog for a walk
4. Put makeup on
5. Eat breakfast

To Do Later Goals For The Day

1. Park one block away from work so I can walk and gain extra exercise
2. Call to make that dentist appointment
3. Pick up dry cleaning before going home from work
4. Hand in report to manager
5. Go to gym to do cardio for one hour
    - ✓ Every night cross off the goals achieved for that day.
    - ✓ Create these lists each and every morning.

Getting in the habit or writing out goal lists has a number of emotional benefits. For one, writing the goal list helps you take control of your focus. Most of us are "other" focused. Sadly many of us spend most of our time thinking about what others think, feel, need, want, or expect from us. Writing goals each morning helps us funnel our attention back into our own awareness of Self. Making a habit of creating goal lists is a practice that should not be undervalued.

Goal lists can be utilized for an array of situations. Let's say you are having trouble with a parent or sibling and you need clarity when it comes to your relationship. Your goal lists might look like:

Immediate Goal List

1. Do a morning meditation on calming the mind.
2. Walk for a half hour before work.
3. Journal about how I feel about my feelings surrounding this issue with Mom.
4. Remind myself that I matter, and repeat this mantra over and over in my mind.
5. Make myself a nutritious breakfast and skip coffee because I am feeling anxious.

To Do Later Goal List

1. Call Mom on the way home from work and set up a time to have our much-needed conversation.
2. Do another meditation before our call to clear my mind.
3. Before calling Mom, write out all the points I want to make.
4. Decide how much of my time I am willing to give this phone call, and then set my timer.
5. As soon as I get off the phone with Mom, no matter how it turns out, I am going to buy myself a bouquet of flowers.

Creating goal lists helps us take control over our focus, clarifies our intention, and allows us to be more present in the Now. The habit of creating goal lists allows us to tap into the feeling of growth and expansion. With the feeling of growth and expansion comes the sense that we are no longer stuck in the past. Learning to push oneself forward and appreciate the ability to create one's own forward-moving momentum creates a sense of empowerment we may have never known before.

One day perhaps your goal list might look like this:

Immediate Goals

1. Drop the dog off at pet hotel.
2. Transfer money to the vacation account.
3. Pack overnight bag.
4. Check my flight.
5. Call limo to verify time for pickup.

To Do Later Goals For The Day

1. Get a massage at the hotel spa.
2. Relax and read my new book by the pool.
3. Tonight, enjoy a wonderful dinner in hotel restaurant.
4. Dance in the ballroom.
5. Use the sauna before bed.

AIMS ACHIEVED BY INCORPORATING
GOAL-SETTING HEALING STRATEGY

The benefits of incorporating this simple strategy step into your every-day life are limitless. The flow this exercise creates is magical. ACoAs tend to get stuck in never-ending loops in their minds. This exercise helps interrupt those loops in a very basic, no-nonsense way. When you write down even some of the mundane things you need to do every day, it is the conscious, decisive act of writing down that goal—in addition to the deliberate completion of that goal—that helps the brain feel more in control. The idea is to help the brain feel more deliberate, focused, and in control over its ability to make a decision and follow through. In time, you will have created enough positive flow that it will become the norm for you to desire to do even greater things.

This strategy was designed to help you learn how to use goal lists for the purpose of creating flow in a tangible way, and to enhance your feeling of control by consciously taking time out of your day to appreciate the achieving of those goals.

6. Repeat-Recycle-Recreate

Childhood Vibrational Patterns

If it is true that like attracts like, then it makes complete, although sad sense that as adults many of us have attracted vibrational beings into our lives who are very similar to our parents or siblings. As children we were sponges, absorbing and aligning ourselves to the energy of the beings who raised us. Defenseless to what impressions they were making upon our spongy minds, we absorbed well. And this of course, Dear Ones, is not our fault.

It is said that birds of a feather flock together, and so it is true for the emotionally abused child from the dysfunctional, non-nurturing home. When you experience emotional abandonment:

- You are brainwashed to avoid seeking guidance from the Self.
- You have no conscious understanding of the Self.
- You model your parents' behaviors.
- You model your parents' beliefs.
- You do not feel heard.
- Your perceptions are minimized and/or denied.
- As an adult you may be overly sensitive to criticism, in fear of others threatening your right to your own perceptions.
- You attract your unique, although broken, concepts of love.
- If Mom enabled, then you probably enable poor behaviors in lovers, friends, and coworkers.

- If Dad was avoidant and emotionally unavailable, then you probably tend to attract partners with similar emotional set points.
- If you were frustrated by your mom, and by your inability to connect to her, you may attract partners who frustrate you and with whom you are unable to truly connect.
- If your family lacked respect for one another's feelings, you may be attracting others into your life who show little concern for your emotional well-being.
- If your mom screamed, yelled, and threw hissy fits instead of consciously choosing boundaries to direct her life, you may be a chronic complainer rather than a deliberate creator.
- When your parents are disconnected from their emotional selves, they are unable to model that connection for you, and so you do not naturally trust the guidance that comes from within.
- Today you may be full of anger, rage, resentment, sadness, guilt, shame, and feel stuck.
- Today you may react quickly when you sense you are not being heard.
- Today you may be taking out all of your frustrations on those closest to you, while presenting a different persona to those who you do not live with.
- Your family may see you as difficult to talk to, explosive, and/or withdrawn and without needs.

Energetic Leaks Caused By Denial

Inconsistent nurturing impacts a child's ability to trust the Self. Inconsistency is a common norm in dysfunctional homes. If one day we were nurtured when we fell, and on the next day we were called clumsy and were yelled at for crying, the inconsistent response by our parents hindered our ability to develop trust in others as well as in our personal worth to be cared for.

If our feelings were ignored, or if we were never asked about our day, the messages we received from our parents were, "I am not enough. I am unimportant. How I feel is irrelevant."

How can I know what I want if the authorities in my life were indifferent to the "I" or the "me" that I am/was?

Bonds are energy circuits. There needs to be flow and consistency in energetic circuits in order for the current to be strong. When we are raised by beings who live in denial, and our perceptions of reality are questioned or ignored, great energy leaks occur within our being. Unable to connect our perception to theirs, we are often forced into worlds of inner delusion, in an attempt to try to make sense out of what we feel intuitively does not make sense.

As children we wonder to ourselves:

- Am I crazy?
- Maybe I am wrong.
- Maybe I didn't see that.
- Maybe I am wrong for feeling that Mom should leave Dad.
- Maybe my brother didn't mean to push me down the stairs.
- Maybe Daddy isn't drunk.
- Maybe Mom and Dad aren't fighting.
- Maybe Mommy isn't having an affair with Uncle Bob.
- Maybe Daddy isn't touching me inappropriately.
- Maybe it's okay that husbands hit their wives.
- Maybe I am crazy for feeling like there is something wrong.
- Maybe I am selfish for wanting Mom to leave Dad.

- Maybe I am selfish for wanting my brothers and sisters to just leave me alone.
- Maybe I am selfish for asking for a birthday party.
- Maybe I am bad for fighting with my sister.
- Maybe I am stupid.
- Maybe I am not enough.
- Maybe they'd be better off without me.
- Maybe they are smarter than me.
- Maybe I don't deserve to have these feelings.
- Maybe I am selfish for wanting to talk about my feelings.
- It must be me. I must be crazy or something because everyone else in my family seems to be okay with what is happening in our home.

Unable to emotionally connect with our parents hindered our ability to love ourselves, trust our perceptions, and attract healthy others as adults. Because we were dependent upon the very people who denied what was truly happening in our homes, and what consequences our living environments had on us as the innocents, many of us were forced deep inside our own minds, far away from the blistering pain feeling unloved created. Many of us dissociated from our emotional selves, because being in the moment and in touch with how painful it felt to be disconnected from the people we loved allowed us to find some sense of solace. Unfortunately, although disassociating helped us survive the pain in the past when we could neither fight or flee, today we may be struggling to reconnect with that very aspect of our Self we were forced to abandon in order to survive so long ago.

We Cannot Continue To Abandon The Emotional Self And Expect To Be Okay

Children are born with an innate need to bond with mother and father.

This bonding is crucial to survival. Feeling connected to our family (tribe) ensures we will be cared for, and will develop the ability to care for the members of our family later on in life. When this need to feel seen is frustrated by a dysfunctional family system, the children of this system internalize the rejection, perceive Self as corrupted, and are unable to form healthy perceptions of the Self.

Very often this need to feel seen by those who rejected us within our family is so strong that throughout our life we continue to seek validation from energy beings similar to those who shunned us as children. It is not our fault we are biologically wired to feel seen by the ones we love, or by beings who energetically represent the ones we love later on in our life. In order to overcome this biological drive to bond with dysfunctional others, we need to use our ability to tap into higher realms of consciousness to access reason as well as logic into our thought processes.

Today we may be unconsciously seeking to bond with similar energy beings from our pasts.

It is completely innate and appropriate for a child to wish to feel connected to his/her parents. This feeling of connectedness, although invisible, is as real as any other non-visible energy stream there is. Although we cannot see the energy that streams through our cable lines, we believe it exists. Because our brains witness the byproduct of conducted energy—the images on our televisions—we believe wholeheartedly that the energy exists in spite of not being able to see the flow of invisible energy.

*Why do we seek to complete the bonds with unavailable others later on in life?*When we are unaware, we are unaware we are unaware. From this blind-to-vibrational-Self vantage point, we can only attract what we are on a vibrational level. Whatever emotion/feeling we identify as love is the emotion/feeling we seek later on in life through our adult relationships, and label as love. Our seeking, of course, is not conscious. Instead, we are attracting what we know, on a vibrational and invisible level.

Personal Story

As a little girl I was very aware that my mother and I were NOT connecting. As if it were yesterday I can still feel the shadow that blanketed me as a child. It was a shadow that made me feel like I was not enough. This feeling of not enough-ness was one I could never shake. From time to time I could escape its grasp by floating away on an OCD trip that involved counting numbers, or pulling hair out of my head. But for the most part, this shaming shadow was a familiar companion.

The love I had for my mother was not healthy. More than any other emotion, I ached for my mother. I ached for her touch, her hug, her acknowledgment, her validation, her acceptance, and even her eye contact. I remember obsessing over the possibility of finally gaining her affirmation. If my family lived in a fishbowl, I felt like the fish on the outside of the bowl, observing the members of my clan going about business as normal. In my mind I was the problem. I was the cause of this gap between my mother and me, and this ache was my fault.

Now I understand that it was no coincidence that I attracted a husband who was emotionally blocked. From the eye-in-the-sky perspective, I can piece the puzzle of my life together, almost with my eyes closed now, as I have learned to appreciate the vibrational order that has divinely orchestrated the unseen. My first marriage, as painful as it was, simply represented the law of cause and effect. Love was ambiguous and something I needed to prove myself worthy of. It would not have been possible for me to attract a spouse who was emotionally available and who did not enjoy withholding validation from his partner.

On a vibrational level, I was attracting my understanding and perception of love. Deeper, I am certain that by attracting my mother's emotional twin, I was unconsciously seeking to complete that crucial initial energy bond, and somehow shake that heavy shadow. Similar to how I felt as a child, the home my husband and I first built never quite felt like a home at all. I consistently felt like an outsider, trying to prove herself worthy of the clan she had married into. And although three decades had passed since my first attempts at sealing that bond, on a vibrational level, I was still a three-year-old emotionally abandoned little girl seeking to connect with her perception of her mother's energy.

Not Accustomed To Things Making Sense

Most of us grew up in homes where things just never made any sense.

- We were children, yet many of us felt like the adults.
- We thought we should have felt loved, but we always felt more like we were in the way.
- We thought that Mom had the right to leave Dad, but she said she couldn't.
- We thought Dad should wake up and go to work like other dads, but he complained he couldn't.
- We thought our house should be clean, but it wasn't.
- We thought we had a right to sleep in peace, but our family was explosive.

- We thought we should be able to ask our teachers for help, but we were conditioned to fear telling our truth.
- We thought we had a right to be angry, but our parents ignored our feelings.
- We thought we should be able to talk about our feelings, but we were mocked, criticized, or beaten whenever we tried to open up.
- We thought our moms and dads should only have one personality, but often noticed they had separate personalities for different situations.
- We thought we had a right to defend ourselves if our parents accused us of something we didn't do, but we were programmed to believe otherwise.

As adults many of us may be attracting beings who are emotionally unavailable and who confuse us. We may be so accustomed to feeling "off" as a result of being raised by the psychologically unfit that we do not have the programming to combat other's nonsensical ways. Therefore, we tolerate being manipulated and controlled.

It helps us to remember that when we were children we were programmed to fear other's rejection, and most of our relationships were littered with confusion. Fearing abandonment and rejection, while at same time experiencing confusion as a norm when it comes to relationships, puts us three balls behind the eight ball as adults *until* we become conscious of our unconscious patterns of thoughts and beliefs. Becoming aware of our vibrational set points and early incomplete bonding issues allows us to work in the conscious realm to begin healing what needs to be confronted. Knowing that we are attracting similar energy beings to our parents helps us figure out what it is we need to heal that is causing us to attract unhealthy energy beings into our adult lives.

The next strategy step is designed to help you become more aware of what needs to change.

Strategy Step
The Three Healing A's

Awareness, Assimilate, and Allow

Goal:

The goal of this exercise is to help you become more conscious of patterns in your behaviors and thoughts so you can then assimilate that information and allow new ideas to take hold, effectively breaking unwanted patterns of thoughts.

For instance, if you generally are triggered when someone criticizes you, and you tend to obsess over what criticism you have received, this exercise will help you become aware that you obsess and help you see that pattern and also assist you to develop a healthier pattern to diminish the amount of energy you spend obsessing over something you cannot control.

You will need:

- Fifteen minutes at night before bed
- Journal
- Pen
- Sacred space

Part One:

Awareness

Before going to bed, go to your sacred space and take your journal and pen with you. Once in your sacred space, sit or lie down and begin taking deep breaths. Do deep breathing for about five minutes or until your mind has begun to quiet down. Once the mental chatter has quieted a bit, begin rewinding the day's events in your mind.

Ask yourself these questions:

- During the course of my day, when was I the most unaware?
- During the course of my day, when do I think I overreacted?
- During the course of my day, when do I think my childhood programming got the best of me?
- During the course of my day, when was I most likely acting out of my childhood programming?
- During the course of my day, who do I think triggers the most childhood responses in me?
- When do I feel the most vulnerable?
- What people in my life do I put ahead of my own Self?
- Whose needs do I make more important than my own needs?
- Who in my life do I know, on an innate level, does not really care about what I am feeling?
- Who in my life do I enable to bully me, or negate my needs?
- Where did I allow myself to perceive myself as powerless today?
- When did I feel the most childlike today?
- When did I forget that I am an adult today?

Write the answers to these questions in your journal.

Part Two:

Assimilate

To break the pattern of the Three Deadly R's (recycle, recreate, repeat), we must learn to take responsibility for what data our brains are playing with. When we were powerless as children, we had no choice.

Whatever data our parents, peers, teachers, and religious authorities spewed about us is the data our sponge-like brains absorbed as information. Needing to "fit in," our minds assimilated the dysfunctional data and created belief systems, which became like blueprints in our minds.

Until we write new blueprints, we will repeat, recycle, and recreate new relationships and experiences that will be built upon our family-of-origin's blueprint.

Recovery allows us to write our own set of life plans!

This part of the exercise is about learning to process your new reality. Spend at least ten minutes per day rewinding the course of the events of your day in your mind, and especially before bed. Reread what you wrote in your Awareness exercise and spend time pondering your findings. The more time you give your calm mind to objectify where it fell into old patterns of thought, the easier it will be for your subconscious mind to get on board and help break the old mental patterns.

Pain Versus Pleasure

The brain is wired to avoid pain and seek pleasure. But when you are an emotionally abused child, this wiring can go awry. When you are forced to live in survival, seeking pleasure becomes enmeshed with avoiding pain. Avoiding pain becomes our number one priority.

We avoided pain by becoming hypervigilant. Always on guard in fear of the next verbal, physical, or sexual assault, many of us are unaware we do not seek healthy, pleasurable experiences today. Instead, most of us are stuck in never-ending loops of hypervigilance, control, and disappointment, because we are repeating, recycling, and recreating our old childhood experiences.

Our brains are under the impression they are doing us a favor. Because so many of us lived in war zone-like circumstances, our brains believe we must absolutely stay on guard for the next attack. It is not our brain's fault that it is wired to avoid pain. Our brains are actually trying to keep us safe. The problem is, we just haven't spent enough conscious time in awareness of the fact that we are not six years old anymore, nor have we assimilated this awareness long enough to break our mind's well-intended pattern.

Part Three:

Allow

Now that you have rewound your day and helped your brain objectify its programming, and you have successfully spent some time assimilating the data that is running in your mind, you are now in a heightened state of consciousness. From this open-minded vantage point, you are going to begin creating new future desired outcomes.

Emotionally wounded adults spend almost no time mentally creating the lives they truly desire. Instead, we are caught in codependent mazes that keep us enmeshed, reactive, manipulative, controlled, and powerless. Until we finally STOP and STEP into our right to choose what we do with our mental power, our childhood programming is going to take control over our emotional steering wheel—period! And it DOES NOT have to be this way.

After spending ten minutes assimilating the data you uncovered, you are now going to rewrite a new ending for each of the situations you mentioned in the first part of this exercise.

For example, a completed exercise would follow this type of order:

Part One:

When my mom called today and insinuated that I made stories up about my childhood, I felt myself getting really small. I got a lump in my throat and my chest tightened. When she said, "Oh, stop acting like you had a rough childhood," I reacted poorly. I filled with rage, became silent, and let her steamroll right over me. When we hung up I raced to the pantry and started eating Frosted Flakes cereal. I ate an entire box of cereal after our call, and didn't stop there. I ate ice cream, a bag of pretzels, and even went out to the local deli and bought some chocolate bars too.

I can see that during this event, I was acting out of my programming. My mother's phone call triggered the patterns in my amygdala, and I reacted (powerless like my little six-year-old self used to feel) to that programming. I can see how eating was the way I avoided the rage and powerlessness I was feeling. I can see how not taking control over the phone call, my emotions, and my eating only reinforced all the patterns I am trying to break.

Part Two:

Spend time reading over what you discovered about yourself today.

Part Three:

The next time my mother calls, I am going to take control over the phone call. The next time I hear her minimizing me, I am going to say something like, "You know, Ma, you have a right to your opinion about my perceptions about my life. But in the end, it's my life and I have a right to my perceptions about my childhood. It was MY childhood by the way, not yours. I can understand why you might be threatened by my perceptions. You did the best you could. I get that. But that does not mean I escaped our home without some serious wounds. I am working on gaining emotional control over my life. So now listen, if you want to continue to have a relationship with me, we are going to need some ground rules. It's probably best we do not talk about the past. I respect your right to your opinion, so please respect mine. If, however, you continue to try to control and/or manipulate my perceptions by minimizing them, we will have to reduce our contact. The choice is yours, Mom. So how is the weather there?"

By taking control early, you reduce your chance of being emotionally triggered into becoming Mom's powerless seven-year-old child again. The goal in this scenario would be to state your desire, be direct, and then to get off the topic quickly.

Allowing your mind the opportunity to create new endings to the scenarios from part one of this exercise is like deconstructing and then renovating a new building. You have to see what you don't like, and then think about what you do like, before you can create the building of your dreams. And just like renovating an old building, you are going to need new blueprints to pull it off.

AIMS ACHIEVED BY INCORPORATING THE HEALING A's STRATEGY

This exercise helps the mind reconfigure its perception of pain and pleasure. By taking the time to show the mind that more pain comes from avoiding our truth than it does from confronting our truth, we better our chances of breaking old unwanted childhood programming.

The brain does not know right from wrong. The brain only knows patterns of survival. The brain is wired to keep us safe. What most of us do not realize is our brain does not think. The brain collects information, stores memories, and is habitual in the sense of patterns. It takes an open mind to be able to think about the way one's mind thinks. Until a being is able to learn how to objectify the way he/she thinks, she/he is a puppet on a string being pulled by the strings of his/her childhood past.

Mastering this exercise allows you to heal the old programming, while at same time helps you calm your mind long enough to begin shifting into the creative center of the brain, where you get to summon new ideas that will eventually create fresh blueprints for your new future life.

7. Struggle With Boundaries "Who Am I?"

As adults, emotionally abused children tend to struggle with internal and external boundaries. Because we lived in homes that were verbally, emotionally, physically, and/or sexually abusive, our innocent little minds were preoccupied with trying to thwart off the next attack. Preoccupied by our attempt to avoid pain, we were not blessed with the safety needed to ponder our innate gifts and talents. We do not know our Selves, because during the times in our lives when our parents were supposed to be mirroring positive senses of Self to us—they were ignoring, berating, punishing, criticizing, and abusing themselves, one another, and/or us instead.

Emotionally abused children from chaotic homes are stripped of any sense of security. When mothers and fathers abuse alcohol, drugs, one another, or their children, the home is overwhelmingly toxic. In addition to the constant disordered and unpredictable nature of the home, the people in charge are immature, emotionally ill equipped, and in denial of the core issues altogether. The children born to these zombies are captives. There is no chance at freedom. The zombies in charge hold the keys, and unless the secrets that are held within the home somehow manage to escape, the innocents sometimes become zombies too.

In order to be an adult with healthy boundaries today, we would have needed to feel safe as children. Most of us never felt safe or secure. Many of us lived in constant states of panic. Why? We lived in constant states of panic because our homes were unpredictable. Unpredictability was our home's norm. A lack of respect for one another's emotions, perceptions, wants, desires, and needs created breeding grounds for volatile familial interactions. Blow-ups were part of our everyday realities.

In addition to our families' lack of respect for an individual's right to own their own emotions, many of us were groomed to people-please and care-take for others. Today we may immediately fall into people-pleaser mode whenever someone we know is beginning to get upset.

When we were children we were aware we were powerless when those we loved treated one another poorly. Some of us would fall back into lands of denial, the way we were taught to do, whenever we felt the emotions in our home beginning to flare up.

Because when our emotions got stirred up, they were ignored, and thus we learned to ignore them whenever they would get high; as children we may have tried to control the tempers in our home by falling back into that old pattern as an attempt to calm the waters. We did not know it then, but making-believe everything was okay when we knew on some level it wasn't was us mirroring to others how others had taught us to deny our own charged emotions.

Under these unpredictable, chaotic, enmeshing, fantasy-provoking conditions, it is impossible for an innocent child to tune into Self for the purpose of self-actualization. Discovering Self is far less a priority when survival is our primary concern.

Born to dysfunctional parents, we were taught to DENY our perceptions, emotions, gut instincts, wishes, desires, dreams, and talents. We
were forced to ebb and flow to the erratic whims of others, while our
golden cords to our divine Self lengthened and thinned over time.
Angry, hostile mothers and fathers—blind to their own rage, inap-
propriateness, abuse, aggression, addictions, victimhood, martyrdom,
codependency, and disconnection—caused us to root ourselves psychologically to the chaos of the moments, as being on guard for the
next attack created the need in us to forget looking within. Our inner
eyes were forced to go blind to our innate divine Self. The need to
remain physically safe yanked us from exploring the corridors of our
divine spirits, and so, we grew roots for our own survival.

Many of us are still rooted in those unsettling childhood moments
today. So deeply ingrained is our fear of the unknown, and so intimidated we are at the idea of facing our unknown Self, we are emotionally
frozen in time, while our bodies chronologically age. We are prisoners
of war, although there are no bullet holes in the walls of our home.
This fear-filled existence is denied on many levels, including the lack of
bullet holes on the walls of our home. Nothing feels safe, yet there is
nothing outside of us to confirm our internal reality.

Children rely on outside *tagging*. By that I mean children primarily learn
to tag meanings to situations and events by how their parents react. If
Mommy ignores when Daddy hits her, or when he attacks the children
in the home, then the children in that home are *tagging* that particular
experience in a dysfunctional way. They are *tagging* that experience with
the blanket of denial. They are being brainwashed to tune out and to
somehow stuff the emotions that naturally arise when terror is sensed.

Children from war-zone territories have one benefit
that children from denial-based dysfunctional homes do not.
Children from war zones who are struggling with fear have the
benefit of having their internal realities validated
by their external experience.
When parents deny/ignore their child's inner reality, a great disconnect forms within. This disconnect creates a gap, or a pocket
of pain. Like stagnant water, eventually those gaps and pockets of
pain become impossible to ignore.
The problem is, however, that although the pain is impossible to
ignore, the cause of that pain is invisible to the being's third eye.
The third eye has been tainted by the reflections one sees in the
ignorant parent's eyes.
When a parent reflects disdain or a sense of invisibility back to a
child through the apple of the eye—the apple of the child's eye is
forever soured.
The innocent child does not know that their parent is but merely
reflecting the parent's own ill perception of their own Self
to the child—unconsciously recreating, recycling, and repeating
the parent's own corrupt story of Self and thus infecting the child
with corrupt belief about the Self, which ultimately leads to the
disconnect from Self. This causes angst, guilt, and shame, as well
as creates a breeding ground for all future Self-loathing.

Unfortunately for many of us, these negative Self-loathing patterns have
been set. We have been brainwashed like Pavlov's dogs to deny our right
to experience the trauma we feel on cue. Emotions in us begin to rise,
an internal bell gets rung, and we deny, deny, deny. We avoid, suppress,
rationalize, justify, and recreate our childhood experiences through the
cycles of denial. And until we interrupt that cycle and learn how to flush
those emotions out of our bodies, like we would that stagnant water beneath our homes, we stay stuck recycling our patterns.

*We are a society that has been brainwashed
to run from our miraculous, divine, guiding, truthful emotions.
But we ALL have garbage from the past.
Pretending like we don't won't make it go away.
Sometimes you just have to roll up your sleeves,
pull out the garden hose, grab some bleach,
and deal with scrubbing out the bottom of the garbage can.
It's a dirty job, but when it's complete, the smell is gone!
We must embrace the garbage, and deal with it.
Anything less than that is like denying a gangrenous big toe.
Eventually the infection will consume you if you <u>don't</u> deal with it.
Whoever hast no fear shall not be controlled.
Parents use fear as a weapon to control their children as well as a
way to play out their own denied or repressed
childhood programming.
A free mind leads, not follows.*

<u>Food For Thought</u>

*What might our world look like if fear was no longer used to control in-
nocent children or a society?
What if we were not brainwashed to hate the Self—or one another?
What if instead of being taught we were **not** enough, we were taught that
we were enough, simply because we existed?
What would our projections of others be if we all believed we were good
enough, intuitively?*

Strategy Step
Remembering What I Forgot About Me

Goal:

The aim of this exercise is to help you more clearly define who you are on an authentic level. Adults from dysfunctional homes have been denied the sense of safety needed to progress through the stages of emotional development required to feel safe and secure enough to honor and respect one's Self.

When you are a powerless child who has been forced to live in a state of survival, your priority is to avoid pain. On the contrary, children who are born to healthy parents, who are fortunate enough to feel safe and secure, fluidly pass through required stages of emotional development without getting stuck in any one particular stage. Because children from healthy homes do not need to live in fear, their mind is able to hear the cues that come from within. These cues, or promptings of Self/Spirit, become a roadmap for life. Children from healthy homes who find themselves drawn to singing or dancing more easily follow the guidance that resounds from within, whereas children from dysfunctional homes do not. Children from dysfunctional homes have been brainwashed to deny the Self in covert as well as overt ways.

Many abused children became frozen in time, stuck somewhere between fight and flight. As if to say to themselves, "What will it matter if I complain, or tell the people I love that the way they are treating me hurts? No one will listen. No one will care, and feeling ignored by others will hurt more than if I just ignore how I feel within my own Self." Psychologically terrified to move to the left or to the right, abused children freeze instead. Never have been taught how to tune into the Self, abused children mature chronologically oftentimes completely unaware that they are unaware they are codependent, and blind to their own Self.

This exercise was created to "thaw you out" and to get blood flowing back into those frozen emotional fibers, helping you feel more tangible as a psychologically integrated being—mind, body and soul.

A Note About Children and Suicide

When a child has been stripped of any sense of inner retreat from turmoil he/she cannot control, in some cases children default to suicide as a means to escape. Because children know they are defenseless, when their innocent minds deem the pain intolerable, inescapable, and permanent, children may view death as a more pleasant option than the torture they endure silently on a daily basis. Children may not be able to view what is going on in their life as a temporary situation. A child's pain can be blinding. The blinding pain renders them helpless and unable to perceive their current situation as transient. The need to escape the pain of "now" can become their primary agenda

The human brain is wired to avoid pain. This biological blueprint—coupled with the innocent and fragile thought process of a small child, which includes the absolute need to feel like one belongs—makes for a volatile cocktail when a child is being raised in a home that does not allow for authentic emotional expression, is being neglected, ignored, and/or overtly abused. Void of an unconditional acceptance to feel what one feels, children from dysfunctional homes live in families, houses, bodies, and school communities that are like pressure cookers...without pressure release valves.

For this exercise you will need:

- Quiet, sacred space
- Fifteen minutes
- Journal
- Pen

This entire book has been created to help you recognize and objectify your patterns of thought. Problematic thought and belief patterns are only part of the abused child's healing needs. Abused children are **not** patterned for happiness, and so they do not have the data necessary in their mind's databank to know how to seek it. Instead, abused children generally spend their time avoiding pain as opposed to seeking pleasure.

In spite of any negative childhood experiences, in order to be happy and fulfilled, one must know what one needs to make oneself happy. If I do not know what I want, it is impossible to create a set of goals that might help me achieve that ultimate happiness. Further, if in my whole life I was living in a state of survival, cut off from my authentic Self, it is unrealistic to presume that without consciously addressing this reality head-on I could ever truly make myself happy, or expect someone else to be able to make me happy.

The goal then must be to figure out what kinds of things do in fact impress me with senses of happiness, and to deliberately seek the feelings of joy as indicators to what things and/or experiences might bring me the contentment I seek today as an adult.

- Before you begin, take five deep breaths to help calm your mind.
- Complete the following sentences in your journal.
- Do not be alarmed if you are unable to recall the answers to some of these questions. All of the answers you seek are within you. Some may be frozen in time beneath many layers of thickened fibers, but they are there. With practice you will be able to more easily recall your childhood perceptions.

*Remembering and then connecting the dots between
the mind and the soul's experience happens on an energetic level
through the physical body by way of the chakra system.
Remembering what your inner child felt, experienced, and perceived is crucial to your ability to clear the path for your
Soul's spiritual journey, as well as to be able to live your future life
consciously as your own divine god Self.
Not remembering, not connecting the dots, keeps you stuck in pain,
unconsciously reacting to triggers today like your three-year-old
terrified, powerless little Self.*

1. When I was little my favorite color was…
2. When I was little my favorite thing to do was…
3. When I was little and no one could see me, I remember…
4. I used to get really happy thinking about…
5. I was the happiest when…
6. I used to daydream about…
7. I always wished I could…
8. I remember secretly wishing I could…
9. My favorite thing in the world to eat was…
10. When I knew no one was looking or could hear me, I would imagine…
11. When I was small I used to imagine…
12. The one thing I wanted more than anything when I was small was…
13. I always wished I was older so I could…
14. I wish my mother knew and cared that I liked to…
15. I wish my father knew and showed interest in…
16. I always prayed for a mentor to show me how to…
17. One of my secret goals as an adult today is to become…
18. My dream job would be…
19. If I could I would travel to…

20. If fear was not an issue, I would definitely…
21. If I was not intimidated by other's opinions, I would…
22. I wish people knew I…
23. My favorite time of the year is_____because I…
24. I always wanted to…
25. My favorite music to listen to in the car is…
26. If I could do one amazing thing before I died, it would be to…
27. The greatest part of my day is…
28. I am the happiest when I am…
29. The one thing I would change about my world is…
30. The one thing I really like about me is…

AIMS ACHIEVED BY INCORPORATING THE CONNECTING-THE-DOTS STRATEGY

Mastering this exercise allows your conscious mind the opportunity to connect to your emotional Self in a way you were never permitted to when you were an innocent Dear Little One. This exercise affords you the opportunity to finally validate your emotional experiences and thus your perceptions. When you were a Dear Little One, and no one was checking in with you, you may have felt terrified, powerless, intimidated, confused, forgotten, disillusioned, angry, resentful, and unworthy of love. Most of us who have come from dysfunctional homes were forced to disengage from our emotions as a means to survive. Early on many of us felt abandoned as toddlers, and then found we were either depressed or full of rage as adolescents. Because our perceptions were ignored, we silently learned to believe our perceptions were irrelevant, or somehow wrong. Not being validated has come with a heavy price.

This exercise gives you the ability to access emotions attached to memory, for the purpose of helping you understand what brainwashing has been attached to your locked childhood perceptions of Self as well as others. The purpose of this exercise is to help you integrate your conscious mind with the emotions you were taught to stuff. Doing so helps you create bridges of light that allow the denied emotions/pain to finally be released through the experience of having them validated by a more aware aspect of Self. In essence, we deliberately invoke the power of Higher Self to act as a witness to the pain once experienced in silence.

You are the Way—you are the Light—and you are the Life

8. Struggle With Being Vulnerable And Authentically Intimate

Adult children who have been raised by unpredictable, self-absorbed parents have not been given the emotional and/or psychological attention they needed to formulate an autonomous Self. Much like a field that is intended to one day produce a healthy harvest, a child's sense of Self must be tended to. When parents are unavailable to nurture a child's soul, the child perceives him or herself as unworthy. When a home is littered with humiliation, arguing, embarrassment, harassment, cruelty, and physical abuse, children never relax. Instead they are forced to try to control whatever they can, as the attempt to do so gives them a false sense of power they so desperately need to prevent them from losing themselves altogether.

Many children from abusive homes have had to adjust the way they see themselves so as not to bump against the perceptions of those who were in control of their homes. When I was a child, I believed I was *bad*, which fit my mother's perception of me at the time. Defying her perception was not an option. As sick and as twisted as it is, many of us alter how we see Self in an attempt to fit in or belong. My need to feel *seen* by my mother was so strong, I was willing to adjust how I saw my Self in the hope of possibly finding common ground. In addition to being powerless to her perception of me and how that faulty perception became the groundwork for my faulty perception of Self, it hurt less to believe I was bad than it did to wonder if I were good, and what it was that was so wrong about me she could not accept.

I believe two primary tragedies were created amongst many.

1. I believed I was bad, which caused me to feel terribly ashamed and guilty.
2. I became obsessed with seeking her acceptance as a way to heal the shame and guilt I felt.

I could never have known that my mother's impressions of me had become my own, and that the impressions were false. I could never have known that unconscious tugs of war were to blame, and that my mother's conflicts had nothing to do with me at all. My mother projected her fears onto me, and, I believe, struggled with giving me the love she never received. Born to two alcoholics, my mother was severely neglected. I believe she silently struggled with the demands of motherhood, and may have unconsciously resented the tiny needy newborn I once was. If there is any job in the world that requires a healthy mind, it is the role of mother. Just as wells run dry, so too can the heart.

Codependent Parents

An alcoholic parent generally has an enabling partner. Their tango of codependency imprints us with many negative ideas about relationships. In addition to being emotionally unavailable to their children, because they are so locked in their own codependent dramas, we are at same time not only learning to believe we do not matter, we are being taught enmeshment rather than individualism. In dysfunctional homes, because no one exists independently, and all moving parts work to deny the root cause of the disease in the family, fear of losing control becomes a major factor in relationships with others later on in adult life.

Adult children are full of pockets of pain they have been taught to deny. When they enter into emotional relationships with others, these pain pockets become activated. Many of my ACoA clients report that they feel much more in control when they are not in relationships. All adult children from dysfunctional homes have stuffed wounds behind heavy doors within them. Like boulders that block flowing rivers, these doors prevent the individual from being able to flow love to others as well as accept love from others. Unconsciously terrified to allow others to get too close for a plethora of reasons, many wounded adult children fear losing emotional control and struggle with allowing others to see their wounds. Because authentic love requires the ability to be vulnerable, the fear of revealing the shame and guilt that has been stuffed behind those doors causes many adult children to freeze emotionally.

Some Of The Reasons We Fear Getting Too Close

- Emotional closeness triggers us with PTSD-like reactions because relationships that get intimate carry with them similar feelings of vulnerabilities we felt when we were small and needing to be validated by our mother and father. We are wired to fear the very love and closeness we seek.
- When we were powerless and vulnerable as children, we were open to other's criticism, abandonment, and rejection. Weaved within the desire to be loved is the fear that in exposing our

true selves, we open ourselves up to criticism, abandonment, and rejection again.

- Because our parents may not have flowed love to us in a healthy way, we do not know how to receive healthy love or how to extend it. Instead, we satisfy our thirst for authentic love by settling for what shows up, usually attracting others who are either needy or withholding in the process. We are either suffocated by other's needs for love, or we become so terrified to expose ourselves emotionally, we tend to shut down.

- If our parents were emotionally withholding, we either neurotically seek to take care of others in an effort to gain the other's love and adoration, or we shut down as we were modeled to.

- The intimacy data in our brain is corrupt. We have never witnessed authentic intimacy, and so we are not wired for it. When others in our lives expose their hearts to us, it feels foreign and unfamiliar. Fearing the uncomfortable new feelings, we shut down or push others away.

- No one loved us authentically, which caused us to feel ashamed of ourselves. Loving someone too intimately triggers our shame, and the need to keep it under control.

The Great Conflict

"I need to be validated and loved because I feel so unseen, but if you knew I wasn't worthy you'd leave me for sure, so I will pull you in, then push you away."

Lisa A. Romano

Love becomes a game of cat and mouse. Our patterns of love and friendship mirror the cat chasing the mouse, and the mouse running away. As if the cat was in search of the mouse's love, and the mouse was afraid of being seen, the two play this hide-and-seek game throughout their lifetime. The cats in relationships aren't always seeking love. Sometimes they are seeking negative validation, as they are not wired to seek positive validation—nor do they know how to validate Self efficiently enough to not need to seek outside validation at all. Cats sometimes seek conflict. Because they are not wired for harmony, peace, and calm, loving exchanges of give and take, the conflict serves as a point of contact that is engaging. The contact, although oftentimes a codependent tango of cat and mouse, is the only way a couple may understand how to relate.

In order to stop the cat-and-mouse game within our intimate relationships, we must first stop playing cat and mouse with the Self. We must learn how to be intimate with the Self by learning to embrace our darker sides, the ones we fear others will discover and run away from. The side of us we have been taught to shame has been created through the process of feeling invisible to our caretakers. That angelic, innocent aspect of us that has been ignored, we have deemed as unworthy because of the lack of validation we received for this vulnerable aspect of Self. This is the facet of our Self we must embrace as if embracing a prodigal son.

We Are Not As Bad As We Believe We Are

When you are treated with indifference, like your feelings are insignificant to the authorities in your life, the message is, "You don't matter. You don't count in this equation. Your experience is irrelevant. How you feel is unimportant."

The messages we receive from the outside become the framework for the messages we send to Self on the inside. Like a computer software program, whatever messages we received about our Self and our worth from the outside becomes our ***Language To Self-Program***. If we were taught we were stupid, dumb, ugly, fat, unworthy, inconvenient, unwanted, and so on, our Self-Talk Program sounds like,

I don't deserve to be happy.
I will never have my dream job.
I will never be in a great relationship.
I will never be able to find someone to love me.
I will never be a good mother.
I will never be a good father.
I will never be rich.
I will always be fat.
I will always struggle.
I am not worthy to be happy.
I do not deserve a voice.
I am no good.
I do not deserve love.
I am broken.
Something is innately wrong with me.

Healing the shame that has us stuck recycling this nonsense helps us sweep aside any debris that is still blocking our path to creating intimacy with Self. The next strategy step is designed to help you face the shame and release it once and for all. Then you can begin creating Positive Self-Talk to help increase your inner vibrations and either enhance the relationships you are in, manifest a future authentic love, and/or finally fall in love with your authentic Self.

Strategy Step
Facing The Whispers Of Shame

Goal:

This exercise is designed to help you face the shame, doubt, and guilt the unfair messages you received as a child about Self created in you so long ago. As children born to unaware parents, many of us sadly learned to internalize our parents' lack of understanding, compassion, and empathy. Internalizing their lack of love and support for the open, vulnerable, inno-cent, loving souls we were back then caused our brains to come up with rea-sons for why our parents could not love or connect with us. Unfortunately, the reasons we conjured up have become rooted in our brains.

This exercise will help you weed out those false premises, and help you re-frame your ideas about your Self-worth. Many of us punish ourselves to no end over the most mundane missteps. We do not offer ourselves compassion or empathy because it was never offered to us. We judge Self because we were judged. Healing ourselves from the inside out requires us to face the root causes of the shame.

For this exercise you will need:

- Fifteen to thirty minutes
- Childhood photos of you from 0-12
- 2-3 lovely frames (or more)
- Old family photo album
- Journal
- Pen
- A sweater or sweatshirt you are ready to get rid of
- Cardboard box big enough for the sweater to fit in

Place one of the photos of you from age newborn to seven in one frame, and place another photo of you from age seven through twelve in another frame. If you like, you can place other childhood photos in a collage as well. It is important, however, to have these two main pictures of you in frames, as they will represent your most impressionable years.

The idea is to get a clear, tangible idea of you and your childhood so that during this exercise you are afforded the opportunity to offer emotions to the inner child within you objectively.

Part One:

Finding The Pockets Of Pain Called Shame

Once you have blocked out some time to perform this "thawing" exercise and you are in your sacred space, take five slow, deep breaths to quiet your mind. Put your sweater or sweatshirt on and begin to drop your mental chatter. Your goal will be to quiet the cluttered, disillusioned adult mind so that you can begin hearing the battle cries of your younger soul. You will understand the need for the sweater as we proceed.

It is important to note that from birth to age seven, our parents are our
biggest influencers. Our first impressions of Self
were the results of how we perceived our parents perceived us.
The impressions that were imprinted
onto the invisible screens in our minds
were found in the lenses of our parents' eyes.
What we saw or perceived in their eyes
as they looked upon us
created the framework for what value we placed on the Self.
If eyes are the windows to the souls,

children with dysfunctional parents
read the messages in their parents' eyes correctly.
Dysfunctional parents do not truly know how to "see" their children.
As children we read our parents' eyes correctly.
*The essence of us was **unimportant** to them.*
The critical issue we must attend to today is the meaning we attached to
the experience of feeling unseen.
Whatever value or lack of value we perceived in their eyes for us
defined our first impression of how we saw Self.
The windows to their souls tainted our perception of Self with whatever
impression we witnessed through those windows.
Later on in life, we now see Self through similar panes of glass,
and until we wash those windows with love and with light,
those windows stay murky, and keep us living behind shades of shame.

Finding The Shame

Please take out the first photo of you and begin writing down the answers to these questions in your journal. Imagine you are asking your youngest Self the following questions. Wait for the answers to surface within you. Do not censor them. Accept what comes up without judging or condemning what arrives for you. Sometimes you will receive images instead of words. Try to determine what the image means to you. This is YOUR sacred journey.

- What are you ashamed of?
- Where is this shame coming from?
- Who do you think *gave you* shame?
- Who in your life did you need to know loved you?
- Who convinced you it was not okay to be you?
- Who helped you perceive your Self as unworthy?
- What happened to you that made you fear being joyful?

- Why is it difficult for you to let people in?
- When did you stop letting your heart feel?
- What incident or incidents, if any, do you believe impacted you the most in this period of time from age newborn to age seven that you can recall?
- Who made you afraid to feel?
- Who taught you to feel like your feelings did not matter?
- Who do you wish *saw* you?
- Who did you need to know *saw* the inner you?
- Whose eyes did you look into that made you feel like you did not matter?

Write all the answers to these questions in your journal.

NOTE:

If you are feeling emotional and tears are coming up for you, allow them. Giving your younger soul the PERMISSION to feel the sorrow, sadness, desperation, powerlessness, anger, disappointment, rejection, and abandonment will allow the shame to filter through you like water through cheesecloth.

It is the lack of validation that hurt us when we were powerless. Having no witness to validate our pain caused the most emotional injury. Learning to be the experiencer of the pain as well as the witness of the pain allows us to more fully integrate. Because when we were in pain, we were ignored, or because being ignored was our norm, we, too, have sadly learned to **not** acknowledge how we feel. A key to this healing process is learning how to honor our personal experience by reprogramming our mind to become a witness to the internal experiences we used to ignore.

Look at that photo of you and remember that nothing was your fault. Shame was a thing that was given to you, like someone might pass you a sweater. It is not you. You were an innocent and powerless, angelic soul who was raised by unaware beings. Today you have the power to take that sweater off.

Part Two:

From the ages of seven to twelve, much of our impressions about Self come from our peer groups. As we begin to venture out of the family system, we are forced into school systems, with an entirely new set of rules, ideas, and beliefs to learn from. While our family was our tribe of origin, our peer group represents the second most influential tribe we innately need to feel we belong to.

NOTE:

All human beings have an innate need to feel like they belong. When that sense is corrupted due to dysfunctional family dynamics, the need to feel a part of a flock/tribe may be intensified as the child enters school systems.

Personal Story

So desperate to fit in with my peers, I can remember being as young as seven years old and trying to hold a pen between my fingers like the other more popular girl in my class. I thought that if I held a pen like she did, maybe the other kids would *see* me and perhaps invite me to one of their birthday parties, or talk to me during recess.

During our class photo, I remember sitting next to two very pretty little blonde girls. They were giggling adorably. I remember thinking, *Oh, is this how we are supposed to act when we are having our photo taken? Okay, then I will giggle too.*

Constantly searching for cues for how to be a seven-year-old little girl, I felt lost in a sea of other children my age I was unable to connect to. I did not know that all I had to do was tap into *me*. So ashamed of *who* I thought I was, tapping into that felt like I was tapping into a sewer line. Instead, I searched my classroom for clues that might help me better understand who I needed to be in order to feel a part of this new collection of others.

Please take out the second photo of you and ask your younger Self these questions:

- Who do you remember feeling rejected by?
- Who made fun of you during this time?
- When did you feel excluded?
- How did it feel to not be included?
- Who did you need to be accepted by?
- What did you presume about yourself during this time?
- What incident do you think helped you feel ashamed of your Self during this time?
- What did you need but were afraid or too intimidated to ask for?
- What did you do with all your feelings during this time?
- What did you do with all your fear?
- What did you do with all your disappointment?
- What did you do with all of your sadness?
- What did you do with shame?

Write the answers to these questions in your journal as they come up for you. Again, if any significant memories surface, stop what you are doing and allow the emotions attached to those memories to surface as well. Remember, you have already survived the incident and the wounding. These exercises are merely allowing the energy attached to the memories and the pain associated with them to filter through your chakra system. Once they filter through you, and you give your sub-conscious mind the permission to release them into your conscious space, you will have released many of the energetic bricks that have been holding you down. The main agenda is to witness the pain for the purpose of validating the experience so you can learn to own it, and thus, at your will, release it.

Part Three:

Giving The Shame Sweater Back—Empty Pockets And All

Personal Story

During one of my many attempts at this exercise, I remem-bered a moment in time that I now believe signified one of the core roots for the shame I carried through my life. I was seven years old. I was wearing a red velvet dress. I was sitting on my father's knee. He and I were sketching cartoon characters on a piece of white paper. I felt happy, protected, and even loved by him. I remember the moment I looked up and noticed my mother glaring down at me. Her face was stern. Her eyes were cold. Her lips were tight and her body movements rigid. Her eyes told me she did not want me on my father's lap. I did not know why. I slid off his lap feeling dirty, wrong, and as if I had done something shameful. Mommy did not want me to sit on Daddy's lap, although I did not understand why. I knew this because when I slid off Daddy's lap, Mommy loosened up. It was then that I took my shame to my room like I would a sweater, and lay upon my bed for the rest of the afternoon, feeling dazed, frozen, empty, and lost.

As this memory surfaced in my mind, so, too, did all the emotions that were stored to that frozen point in time that had been locked in my body. While journaling early one morning, the emotions I had shoved deep down inside of me so long ago rose within me. The emotions were so intense I thought I might stop breathing. It felt as if my entire chakra system was becoming unzipped. Although I could not see it with my physical eyes, in my mind's eye I imagined a great white light either coming out of my heart chakra or entering my heart chakra, or perhaps both. My eyes wept heavily as this bright white light surged through my body that early morning. While my family slept in their bedrooms upstairs, buckets of shame began to dissolve as I sat there quietly journaling and sipping on green tea. This occurrence has been one of the most life-changing I have ever experienced. Once my mind allowed itself to witness the silent suffering of the innocent child within me, the shame I had been carrying no longer fit. Observing the inner child I once was, who was once so full of yearning for love, allowed me to have compassion for my Self in a way that afforded me the opportunity to experience true love for the divine, innocent Self.

Learning to have compassion for the innocent little girl I once was proved to be transformational. Actually rewinding my memory for the purpose of bearing witness to the pain of the little girl I once was healed my being on many different levels. In addition to finding compassion for my Self, surprisingly I found compassion for my mom as well. When my mother was a young child, she was sexually abused. One of the men who abused her was a man she trusted. Almost immediately after my chakra system became unblocked that morning, I found myself floating in complete understanding. Without much cognitive reasoning, I understood that my mother had simply handed me the sweater of shame she had worn her whole life, probably since she was seven years old, just as old as I was the day her eyes told me to get off my father's lap.

That miraculous morning I began to understand that all the shame I carried for so long had nothing to do with me. My mom could never have known that she had passed the shame she carried unconsciously onto her own innocent daughter. The shame was not handed to me on a plate. It was transmitted on a vibrational level, received by me, the innocent, impressionable child. From the eye-in-the-sky perspective, I understood my mother and I were both victims.

Once you have completed the above writing assignments, you are ready to go on to step three, where we are going to clearly identify WHO gave us our sweater of shame and all the heavy bricks that are now our pain pockets.

Please answer the following questions in your journal:

- The person who I believe handed me the most shame between the ages of zero to seven was…
- Other people who handed me shame during this impressionable time in my life were…
- The person I believe handed me the most shame between the ages of seven and twelve, who lived outside of my home, was…

- Other people who handed me shame during this impressionable time in my life were…

Part Four:

Once you have identified the people in your life who passed their shame to you, it is time to pass the shame back to where it came.

Label your box with the names of those people you have identified in part three of this exercise.

Part Five:

Once you have labeled your box, take off your sweater of shame and place it in the box on the floor in front of you. Stand up and turn away from the box and repeat out loud the following affirmations:

- I lovingly return this shame from where it came.
- I lovingly release the pain that has come with *your* shame.
- I lovingly release these pockets of pain, and allow Self-love to heal this shame.
- I lovingly release any ideas of me that have me believing I am unworthy.
- I lovingly release any thought form that has made me feel stuck.
- I lovingly release any shame and/or actions I have taken in my life that may have been rooted in running from that shame.
- I lovingly release any shame of not knowing that my younger Self was sowing other people's shame.
- I lovingly release the bondage that has kept the younger soul that was I from being able to feel free.
- I lovingly rebuke shame, as I am learning that seeing myself this way was an illusion.
- I lovingly refuse to wear a cloak of shame any longer.

- I am enough.
- I always was enough.
- I am here to learn, grow, and expand.
- From this day forward I promise to forgive myself when I make a mistake rather than condemn myself when I fall back into the faulty programs and patterns of my subconscious mind.

After you have read the affirmations aloud, place the box behind you. This symbolizes many things.

1. The shame is outside of you—and no longer within you.
2. The shame has been given back to its rightful owner.
3. Your subconscious mind and conscious mind are finally in agreement.
4. The need to feel ashamed of any unresolved shame is no longer an issue.
5. You are no longer stuck in a pattern of resistance.
6. You are now in a state of allowing.
7. Forward-moving momentum has been created.
8. Fear is no longer in charge.
9. There is nothing to fear.
10. You were always enough.
11. You have successfully coped with the shame.
12. You have honored your younger soul's experience.
13. You have honored Self.
14. You have integrated more deeply.
15. Integration has been activated.
16. Healing energy has been created.
17. You are learning how to master your emotions.
18. You are learning to feel your emotions.
19. You are learning how not to fear your emotions.
20. You are learning to love Self.

21. You are tapping into your divine Self.
22. You are learning to clear negative emotional blocks.
23. You are learning to understand how to discipline your mind.
24. You are learning how to focus your attention.
25. You are learning how to confront painful memories and emotions.
26. You are learning how to separate your programming from your deliberate thought processes.
27. You are learning how to take control over how YOU want to feel.
28. You are learning how to parent Self.
29. You are learning to take care of that inner younger you.
30. You are learning to honor your own wounds.

AIMS ACHIEVED BY INCORPORATING THE TAKING-THE-SHAME-SWEATER-OFF STRATEGY

This exercise was designed to help you uncover the pockets of pain you may have had hidden beneath heavy emotional layers of denial and avoidance. Because our brains are wired to avoid pain, many of us do exactly what we should not do when we are trying to heal; we go straight for the spiritually uplifting material and neglect to confront the infections from the past first.

Much like you would not build a skyscraper on a bed of sand, a healing through the head while the toes are massively infected is short-lived at best. The only way to truly heal and transcend is to uncover and successfully allow the emotions attached to the experience to be expressed while consciously choosing to embrace the pain from the past.

In reality, your younger soul has already survived the trauma. The only thing your innocent younger soul was not permitted to do was express and validate the emotions that were attached to the experience. By consciously permitting your being the ability to experience the emotions openly, you are in essence honoring your own Self by giving your younger Self the divine-like validation it was always searching for. It is important to bear witness to our own suffering by seeking the wounded child within.

You, Dear One, are learning to validate your own Self! You are learning to love the Self. You are learning what it means to come into alignment with divine Self. You are learning to accept your divine nature by overcoming human pain caused by not believing in Self.

The more deeply you accept how perfect you really are at your core, the more enlightened you become. The more you shift out of the *I am not enough* mind, the greater your ability to love Self as well as others.

Living an enlightened life requires us to overcome any illusion caused by any other unaware beings we have encountered on our path. Overcoming those illusions requires us to HONOR the human emotions caused by being invalidated on emotional/vibrational/psychological levels. Feeling unseen has corrupted our ability to see Self as divine. Learning to witness the suffering caused by the corruptive brainwashing helps us to integrate and thus feel more valid, real, and authentic.

THIS IS THE PROCESS OF ENLIGHTENMENT, DEAR ONES!

9. Highly Reactive

It is nearly impossible **not** to be *overly reactive* as an adult if you have been ignored, abused, denied, and treated with indifference as a child. Because as adults we have a cognitive understanding that we are "big people" now, we carry with us an illusion of power associated with being a certain chronological age that was created in our childhoods, based on how we perceived abusive adults in our lives. We presume that because we are older now, others should generally do what we want them to do and say what we expect them to say. When we were powerless children, many of us presumed the pecking order had something to do with the tugs of war in our homes that were centered upon control. We may not have understood that at the true core of our family's struggles with power and control was denial.

When parents abuse their authority over us as children, confusion becomes a cornerstone of our fragile realities. Being treated unfairly scrambles our hearts and our minds like eggs. We wonder, *Do my parents love me, or do they hate me? Should I feel this confused? Is this what being a child is supposed to feel like? Why don't I feel happy? Is this what love is? Am I supposed to be this terrified all the time? Do I have a right to be this angry?*

Because dysfunctional parents live in total denial of the abuse they inflict upon their children, and because children look to their parents for meanings to what is happening in their life, when abuse is swept under the rug, children are denied the RIGHT to experience the very NORMAL and appropriate emotions that accompany parental abuse. This causes complete confusion and hinders the child's ability to formulate a healthy identity, as nothing in the home is predictably loving or supportive.

For a child to develop a solid and healthy identity, he/she has to come from a nurturing, stable, encouraging environment with fair and negotiable family rules.

A father can whip his son with a leather belt like he was whipping a wood post and in the next moment ask his son to run down to the corner market for milk. A passive-aggressive mother can snarl at her daughter before the daughter leaves for school, and in the next breath tell her she loves her. At moments that follow abusive incidents like these, children are short-circuiting energetically. It hurts to be physically and/or emotionally abused by the people you love. But it hurts even more when the people you wish you could trust act like no violation has taken place at all.

The messages our tiny brains and hearts perceive about adults sound like this:

- Big people get to make the choices.
- Big people get to be in control.
- Big people's feelings matter.
- Big people punish other people.
- Only big people matter.
- Big people are allowed to be angry.
- Big people have the power.
- Big people are allowed to be physically abusive.
- Big people are allowed to tell other people how they feel.
- Big people are the boss.
- Big people get to tell other people what to do.
- If you're big it's okay to react.

Dysfunctional parents are unaware that their innocent children are assigning a meaning to EVERYTHING in their reality. How our parents treated us defined our identities in many ways. It also defined for us what meaning we assigned to others and our experiences.

Identities Or Labels Parents Help Children Create About Themselves

- I am powerless.
- I am no good.

- I am worthless.
- I have no voice.
- I have no right to feel.
- I have no right to be happy.
- I am not happy.
- I cannot trust my decisions.
- I cannot trust my Self.
- I am needy.
- I am controlling.
- I am a bitch.
- I am a wimp.
- I have no backbone.
- I have no identity.
- I am a shell.

Unpredictability

A huge problem in dysfunctional homes is unpredictability. Forming a sound identity for a child who comes from an abusive home is like trying to pour a concrete foundation during a never-ending earthquake. YOU CAN'T DO IT! A child CANNOT form a healthy sense of Self in a home that is unpredictable. It is impossible, in my humble opinion.

The Self

How can a human being have Self-esteem if the human being does not yet know it has a Self? Most people behave and think like sheep. They get up every Tuesday and do exactly what they did last Tuesday. They react to people and situations without thinking about the myriad of choices they actually do have around a particular circumstance. Without thinking, they falsely presume they are making decisions when in reality many of their decisions have been predetermined by their unchallenged childhood programs.

We all have a Self, but not all of us know the Self. Healing appropriately allows us to peel away any layers of ill thinking or beliefs that prevent us from connecting to the Self. If our parents were aware, stable, loving, and nurturing human beings, then they would have helped us stay connected to our innate Self. If our parents had treated us fairly and we felt safe enough to express our honest emotions, the act of expressing our emotions would have kept the line open to Self.

If we had not been taught to fear expressing our Self, then as adults we would naturally have esteem for this Self. We would naturally seek partners who were emotionally available and nurturing. We would also be emotionally available because we would be VOID of any fear associated with revealing our true Self.

The Link To Low Self-Esteem And Our Reactivity

People with high Self-esteem know they have nothing to prove. Connected to their divine core, they are Self-forgiving, Self-accepting, Self-nurturing, Self-accountable, Self-reliant, Self-correcting, and of course Self-loving. People with high Self-esteem are also non-Self-judgmental and non-Self-critical. They understand that they are a work in progress and that it is normal to make mistakes. Having high Self-esteem is not to be confused with arrogance, narcissism, or one-up type personalities.

When you have esteem for the Self, you naturally respect your emotional well-being. When you respect the Self, you respect your mind space, and seek to keep a state of being calm. People who highly respect themselves are goal-oriented, pleasure-seeking, and chaos-avoidant. To heal our tendency to overreact to everything, one of our main goals is to develop predictable routines that will help us learn to develop the foundation we need to begin working our way back to the Self.

In this next strategy step we are going to go back in time and begin teaching you how to nurture your Self the way you were supposed to be nurtured. You will learn to make your Self a priority. Most importantly you will learn how to rely on your Self for the guidance, nurturance, and validation you seek which becomes the cornerstone of your new healthy sense of Self.

**Healing will require you to replace your old perception of Self,
the one that brainwashed you to believe
you were nothing and powerless,
with an entirely
new perception of Self.**

**Your new perception of Self will be rooted in divinity and truth,
rather than illusions created by other people's delusions.**

Strategy Step
The I Am Mirror Exercise

Goal:

This strategy step was designed to help you reconnect to the Self that has been with you all along, that has merely been covered over by old programming. Much like a fossil that lies beneath many heavy tons of stone, the Self is, was, and always shall be with you. The Self—is YOU!

Before our birth we were merged with Self. Upon our birth we were propelled into a world of illusion created by generations of other's delusions that caused us, for many reasons, to become detached consciously from the

Self. We did so in order to survive. When our physical body can no longer sustain the machine that it is, our Self will merge completely with Source once again.

We have been born to successfully transcend the pain caused by dis-associating from Self, for the purpose of spiritual awakenings and oneness. Pain has forced us to let go of needing to cling to others and to finally seek within for the peace we have longed for through-out our lifetimes. As truth-seekers our journeys will always lead us back to Self.
Just as Buddha and Christ have taught, "I am the way ~ I am the truth ~ I am the life." The Self is the Great I Am.

Whether you believe in oneness or not is a matter of your own particular belief system. The "Great I Am" need not be associated with any religion or spiritual belief system. If you are non-religious and even atheist, the Great I Am is still YOU. Your inner Self—the part of you that feels, thinks, desires, and behaves based on your own unique set of values—is your mighty I Am. If you are put off by any correlation made to Christ or to Buddha, please do not devalue the message found in this strategy step. Take what works for *you*, apply what feels appropriate for *you*, and discard what does not feel right for *you*.

For this exercise you will need:

- Fifteen minutes preferably twice per day, morning and night
- Complete quiet time—no cell phones, no house phone, no dogs/cats/children
- A mirror, preferably full-length (a closet mirror will do)
- A 3- to 4-inch white candle on a stand and matches
- The following list of affirmations you will tape onto your mirror (please rewrite them in your own handwriting as this will

also help your conscious mind reconnect with a higher perception of Self)

- Tape
- A large pillow, mat, or blanket to sit on
- Meditation or instrumental spa music playing softly in the background
- Journal
- Pen

Once you have gathered your items:

- Place the mirror in a room where you know you will absolutely not be disturbed.
- Place the candle in front of the mirror.
- Place the pillow far enough from the candle so as not to catch fire.
- Light the candle and turn off the lights in the room.
- Take the list of affirmations and tape them to the mirror so you can read them aloud.

Affirmation List:

- I Am enough.
- I have always been enough.
- I Am good.
- I have always been good.
- I Am worthy.
- I have always been worthy.
- I Am here; here is where I Am.
- I have always been here.
- My pain was real.
- My pain is real.

- I Am willing to release the pain.
- I Am strong enough to transcend the pain.
- I Am willing to transcend this human experience and merge with the greater part of me.
- I Am willing to trust my inner guidance system.
- I Am my own guidance system.
- I can trust my divine gut instincts.
- I can trust the guidance of the Great I Am.
- I Am the Great I Am.
- I Am safe.
- I Am protected.
- I Am empowered.
- I Am well.
- I Am healthy.
- I Am loving.
- I Am loving me.
- I Am willing to step into my new role as creator of my world, and to let go of any lower identity I have ever clung to.
- I Am no longer a victim.
- I Am the Great I Am.

Once you have rewritten these affirmations in your own handwriting, tape the paper to your mirror and then sit in a comfortable position upon the pillow or mat in front of you.

Take five deep, cleansing breaths to quiet your mind. Once you have quieted your mind, take a few moments to stare directly into the windows of your soul. Behind those eyes resides your inner Self, the Self others taught you that you needed to disconnect from. Be patient with your Self. Oftentimes it can be overwhelming to see Self in a nonjudgmental way.

Sadly for many, it is routine for us to beat up the image we see in the mirror. We fail to recognize how we ourselves perpetuate the cycles of abuse we received as children. We do not take into account all the innumerable and innocuous times we mock ourselves. This exercise helps us become more aware of our own patterns of Self-abuse, and helps us reprogram our perceptions of a new Self as well.

Repeat the affirmations for a minimum of fifteen minutes. In your journal, note any memories or emotions you connected to that you believe you might be able to release. You will find that the more stable you feel in your own being, the more toxic emotions and memories you will be able to release. Allow what comes up to surface, holding steadfast to the concept that within you lies the Great I Am.

Aims Achieved By Incorporating The I Am Mirror Exercise

This exercise is designed to help you feel more stable so that you can finally find the inner peace you may have always been searching for, which allows you to correct your old perceptions of Self. As you discover the reality that you were ALWAYS worthy, and that your inner Self was ALWAYS with you, you will find it much easier to just be you. The need to seek other's approval will diminish, and your fear of what others think of you will no longer guide your decisions through life. Fear will lose its hold over you, and it will become so much easier for you to laugh, let go, and have fun.

The brain does not know what it is doing wrong. Most of our unchallenged perceptions of Self are the result of other delusions about life as well as denial. This exercise challenges the illusions as well as any delusions you hold about Self, for the purpose of creating ease in the body as opposed to dis-ease. Easing you out of your old perceptions and into new perceptions assists you on your healing journey.

The bottom-line agenda of this exercise is to get you to connect to your divine Self, and to help you release any attachment you had to a false self. The more time you dedicate to this strategy, the greater your connection to your divine Self. Once you feel connected to your divine Self, you will then move through life without attachments to temporary illusions, like other people's opinions, actions, or even other people. Everything in life is temporary, so to attach to anything is to confuse the mind.

Once you are connected to your divine Self, honoring Self begins to make more sense. Now connected to Self, you can experience respect for Self, and finally understand what it means to have high Self-esteem. Living from Higher Self implies you no longer have anything to prove. You are enough, you always were enough, and now your heart, mind, and body all agree!

This is called integration, my friends! When the subconscious mind no longer battles the conscious mind, energy flows unobstructed, anxiety diminishes, love energy flows and attracts, and peace is finally found. We discover we no longer react to everything in our environment. We value our peace, allow others to set sail upon their own sacred journeys without expecting them to do what we want them to, and focus more intently on our own desires with hope in our hearts.

10. Neurotically Avoid Pain Rather Than Seek Pleasure

While researching how this thing called my "brain" worked, I discovered something simple, yet amazing. Although I had learned about the term in my college psychology classes, it wasn't until I dug into breaking the codependency programs embedded in my mind did I decide to pick apart this brain fact.

It seems human beings are wired to seek pleasure and to avoid pain. This is an awesome design if the being operating the program has not come from a dysfunctional home. If a being has been brainwashed to deny the Self, and as an adult still lives in a state of survival, this system goes awry. Frozen adult children from dysfunctional homes may be caught in endless loops of pain avoidance, unaware they are unaware they are not actively seeking pleasure. Adult children perceive the ability to control how much pain they are in as pleasurable.

When The Feedback System Goes Awry

Consider a two-year-old boy who seeks to be consoled because he has bumped his head on a kitchen counter. This child's primal need will be to seek comfort. He is in pain. He does not know how to relieve the physical pain and naturally seeks one of the adults in his life for some form of relief. If this child has been born to healthy, well-adjusted adults, the child will be tended to lovingly, consoled quietly, and perhaps aided by a few cubes of ice applied in a nurturing way by his mother or father.

The child's experience is one that has taught him to seek Mother and Father when he experiences physical pain or trauma. Mommy and Daddy are safe and he can trust them and his impulse to reach out to them. The deepest program may be that this child can trust his right to feel, express, and be validated by others. There are no energy blocks created. From the moment the trauma is perceived, the chain of events flows naturally until some sort of resolution. In spite of the original source of trauma, the child's energy has not become blocked, and instead has found resolve.

What if this little boy's mother was drunk, or was a narcissist? What if this little boy's father had little impulse control and had had a hard day at work? What if this little boy's parents were always arguing? What if this little boy's house was full of dysfunctional adults? What if this little boy's parents were preoccupied with a sibling's addiction? What if this little boy was shoved to the ground for crying like a baby by the parents he sought solace from? What if every time this little boy cried, he was yelled at, hit, punished in some way, or ignored?

How would this little boy's brain interface with the pleasure-versus-pain principle?

If this child experienced deeper pain from being ignored, punished, hit, or screamed at when he cried than he did from the physical bump to his head, his brain would seek to avoid the deeper emotional pain in the future. Before long this child might develop a pattern that links his own physical and/or emotional pain to even more excruciating pain when considering to express that pain. Naturally he would then seek to deny his pain to others, in fear of what additional pain might come from expressing his own suffering.

It is not difficult to comprehend why children from abusive homes deny their feelings, wants, needs, and desires.
Sometimes it just hurts less to be real.
Denying one's internal experience of pain may be the only thing an innocent child can control.
Denying one's internal experience of pain becomes a way in which the brain can avoid deeper pain.
Children from dysfunctional homes have never felt safe enough to seek truly pleasurable experiences. Because their homes were unpredictable, it may have hurt less *to not want*.

Again, when we consider the organic wiring of the brain and its innate need to avoid pain, it is not difficult to understand why so

many abused children struggle with giving themselves permission to want more than what shows up.

It's simply too risky.

If the brain is wired to avoid pain, we must presume it can somehow prioritize pain.

If a child perceives a deeper sense of pain from being ignored when hurt, then we can presume the child will wish to ignore that experience in the future.In the future, this child will learn to disengage from his/her own pain—as well as his/her innate need to feel as if he/she belongs.

It will hurt less to stuff, deny, repress, suppress, or minimize one's internal experiences.

The consequences are devastating, as it is unnatural for beings to deny internal experiences.

Disassociating from pain becomes a way of life.

It is like living with nails in your feet, and acting as if you have no experience of pain.

You pretend you don't see or feels the nails in your feet.

The people you love pretend they don't see the nails in your feet or sense your pain.

You have been taught that pointing to the nails in your feet makes others angry, and sometimes they even push you away.

So, you slowly learn to live with the pain, and dissociate from your right to point to the nails in your feet.

You don't matter.

Your pain is not real.

It is not valid, or at least that is what you have presumed as a means to survive in the moment, day to day.

Consider the adult child from a dysfunctional home who has been programmed for years to seek pleasure by way of avoiding pain by disassociating with his/her own pain.

Imagine the consequences this being suffers as an adult, as he/she attracts other adults into his/her life who are similar to those who abused him/her when he/she was a child.

Imagine the loop this adult child might be caught in as they:

a) attract similar energetic/vibrational adults into their lives

b) associate pleasure with disassociating with their own pain

c) exist void of boundaries

d) move through life feeling unworthy

e) associate pain with expressing their true selves

f) don't ask for help because they have presumed what is wrong is them, and that is a matter of fact

g) don't ask for help because they are unable to objectify the problem (they are the problem).

The people this adult child loves live in denial, so all causes of pain are denied, thus making it all but impossible to be able to objectify a causative agent for the pain.

Adult children from dysfunctional homes sometimes seek parental validation well into their parents' older years, unaware they are caught in an impossible loop.

The well-intended organic wiring of the brain goes rogue when in the body of an innocent, powerless child who has been born to dysfunctional caretakers.

How An Abused Child Might Seek Pleasure And Avoid Pain

When you are a child who has not been born to parents/caretakers who honor the little being that you are, your needs go unmet. Although you might be fed, clothed, and enrolled in school, there is a deep emotional gaping hole within your soul that others do not acknowledge. If you are made fun of for crying and/or for having a need, you will quickly learn to flee deeper into your Self, as you have learned the outside world is not safe.

It is not uncommon for abused children to spend time alone. Many of us discovered that being alone hurt less than it did to spend time with others. We did not know that it was fear that was driving us into solace. All we knew was that every so often we needed to escape the emotional torment being aware of *not belonging* created within our being.

In my opinion, the anxieties so many of us experienced were energy blocks. Not feeling like we were valued, loved, or wanted inhibited our ability to flow energy to others or to have energy flow back to us. It is unnatural to not be able to flow love to others or to have that love flow back to us. When this ability goes awry, the chakra system experiences energetic blocks and glitches. I believe these blocks are what the body experiences as disease and the mind may interpret as unnamable anxiety.

Abused Children Seek Pleasure By Avoiding Pain

Many abused children have learned to give up. After many attempts to gain our parents' love, affection, validation, and empathy, abused children sometimes slip into pits of despair. Life is about survival and not joy. Happiness and contentment belong to *other* people—people we presume are more deserving for imagined or unknown reasons. It is far less painful to sit in our rooms and fantasize than it is for us to dare risk being teased, hit, ignored, or to witness another violent episode between our mother and father.

It is not uncommon for abused adult children to develop bizarre coping skills. Many of my clients have shared similar stories to my own that detail how they, too, discovered ways to be "taken away" from their internal emotional torture chambers. To help me fade from my anxieties, I would count letters to sentences I heard others speak, and also memorize license plates. These are just two games my mind would play to help me distract myself from the overwhelming, diseased emotions I experienced as a result of the myriad of energy blocks I experienced as a child.

Healing The Codependent Mind That Has Been Corrupted By Brainwashing

Below is a short list of some of the unconscious, limiting beliefs abused adult children carry with them into adulthood. It is important to note that we might have built our lives on these faulty ideas. To heal will require us to become aware of the unconscious beliefs, as well as to confront them and create new ones that empower us rather than set us up for continued failure.

- I need other's validation to be happy.
- I need to be liked by others.
- Others need to approve of me.
- I am no good without a partner.
- I am not worthy unless someone else sees worth in me.
- I must please others.
- I must stay in my relationship even if I am unhappy.
- I have no right to be happy.

- I don't deserve to be happy.
- I am not good enough.
- I deserve to be unhappy.
- I am not capable of living on my own.
- I cannot take care of me.
- I cannot take total responsibility for my finances.
- I need to take care of someone in order to be worthy of their love.
- I am faulty if others do not like me.
- I am not attractive.
- I cannot reveal my true Self.
- Others will not accept my true Self.
- It is not safe to tell the truth.
- I deserve to be unhappy.
- I am not pretty enough to be treated well.
- I don't make enough money for a woman to find me attractive.
- Society makes the rules about beauty.
- I am not worthy of love unless I make a lot of money.
- I don't deserve a happy relationship because I don't make a lot of money.

Strategy Step
Seek the Belief and Find Relief

Goal:

The goal of this exercise is to help you find the corrupt beliefs that have been preventing you from seeking pleasure and joy in your life. This strategy is designed to address specific areas of your life and help you uncover those anchors that have you feeling weighed down. We now know why those anchors have been created.

1. *Limiting beliefs keep us feeling safe in familiar comfort zones.*
2. *Limiting beliefs require no risks.*
3. *Limiting beliefs justify our reasons for not confronting our perceptions of Self.*
4. *Limiting beliefs allow us to not have to deal with change.*
5. *Limiting beliefs keep us stuck, but also protect us from feeling vulnerable.*

This strategy was designed to help you uncover your limiting beliefs about Self, and to help you discover what areas in your mind are most corrupt with dysfunctional programming. Limiting beliefs are like ceilings. Although your potential is limitless, a limiting self-belief will snip your spiritual wings. In order to become boundless, we must identify the mental anchors that are preventing us from soaring like the angels we truly are.

By clearly identifying a limiting belief, we get to address that particular area of our lives more directly. When we challenge the belief, we ease closer to learning to allow ourselves to begin seeking joyful experiences. By challenging the limiting beliefs that have been created in an attempt to help us seek pleasure by avoiding pain, we successfully learn to cut the chains to those psychological anchors to our pasts. Uncovering the limiting belief provides us with the awareness to push through our mental ceilings.

For this exercise you will need:

- Large Post-it notes or sheets of paper to write on
- Black marker
- Journal
- Pen
- Sacred space
- Ceiling you can reach

Part One:

For this part of the exercise, you will be addressing eight key areas of life by asking open-ended questions that are designed to help you uncover many of your unconscious limiting beliefs. Oftentimes we do not even realize that there are limiting blueprints we have attached our unconscious identity to.

For instance, as a child I routinely heard my father say, "Ya know, money doesn't grow on trees." I remember being about seven years old, thinking, *Yeah, it does. Money is made from paper, and paper comes from trees.* Of course I could not say that at the time. I was intimidated by my father's need to be right, and had learned to fear challenging him or my mother.

My father gave my mother a strict weekly budget. Frustrated, she did her best to meet the demands of our family with the little money he allowed her each week. Living with such tight restrictions on money programmed me to fear spending money. Money was tied to fear and lack, not joy and abundance. It took much patience and commitment to challenge the internal ingrained beliefs in my mind that weren't even mine.

The eight areas of life we are going to be addressing are:

1. Focus. What are you focusing the most of your mental time on, or on whom?
2. Career. What meanings have you attached to your career?
3. Family. What role are you playing for your children, siblings, or parents?
4. Love Life: What role are you playing out in your primary relationship?

5. Physical Body: What perception do you have about your physical body?
6. Social Friendships: What role are you playing out with your closest friends?
7. Money: What does your relationship with money look like?
8. Legacy: How do you think others will remember you?

Please answer the following questions.

Focus

- I believe my free time should be about...
- I spend my free time...
- My free time is usually spent...
- When I am alone I tend to think about...
- In my free time I am usually...

Career

- My career choice was about...
- I chose this career because...
- When I think about my career I feel...

Family

- My primary role in my family of origin is...
- I believe my parents think/thought of me as...
- My siblings and I...
- My children perceive me as...

Love Life

- My love life looks like...
- My love life makes me feel...
- I believe love...

Physical Body

- I see my body as...
- My body makes me feel...
- I think my appearance...

Social Friendships

- I hang out with...
- I spend time with...
- I usually end up going out with friends when...
- My friendships are...

Money

- I think money is...
- Money...
- Money will...
- Money can...
- My relationship with money looks like...
- My family taught me that money...
- People with a lot of money...
- Rich people...

Legacy

- I think people will remember me as someone who...

- If I died today my friends would say I…
- I always thought that my life would help me…
- I would like people to remember me as someone who…

Part Two:

Beliefs By Design

Look at the answers to these questions in your journal. They will reveal crucial information to you about any limiting beliefs you may have about the key areas of your life.

Because this exercise reveals different information to each individual person, the answers to these questions will be unique, and so will the new challenging beliefs you will create.

In your journal take time to create a new set of beliefs that will challenge the old unconscious beliefs you have just discovered through your open-ended question exercise.

Once you have created your new set of unique beliefs, write them down on a Post-it or a large piece of paper and tape them to the ceiling of your sacred space. The ceiling represents the old programming, and the new beliefs represent your new belief system; the one you are customizing to suit your own desired future life's outcome.

Below are some examples of new beliefs you may want to consider adopting.

Spend at least fifteen minutes during your day lying on your back, looking up at these new sets of beliefs, and repeat them out loud. Allow your imagination to create images of you living your life through these new sets of beliefs. Imagine yourself creating a life that never puts a ceiling on how much money, love, peace, contentment, or fun you deserve to experience.

1. Focus

If you discover that most of your free time is spent obsessing about someone else, you will need to challenge the belief that has you unconsciously tying your mental energy to others rather than to yourself.

On your Post-it note, you would write a challenging new limitless belief to help you correct the belief that has you wasting your precious time and energy focusing on things you cannot change.

Possible new challenging beliefs might be:

- I can flow mental energy my way.
- I can worry about me.
- I can think about what I want.
- I can let go of obsessing about others.

2. Career

If you chose your career because of practical reasons like security or health insurance, and you are not feeling fulfilled in your job choice, you might be spending a whole lot of time cursing the job you've chosen. These limiting attitudes will only add to your feeling "stuck" and out of control.

Possible new challenging beliefs might be:

- I don't have to hate this job.
- I can focus on what's right about this job.
- I am thankful this job supports me.

- I am grateful for the job security.
- I can always start looking for another job.
- I have a right to find a job that I really like.
- I can start working on my dream job right now.
- Work can be fun.
- Work can be exciting.
- I can have a career I love and feel secure as well.
- I can have it all.

3. Family

If you feel taken advantage of by your family, or if you are struggling with feeling obligated by their expectations of you and you do not challenge the beliefs that are putting other people in control over your life, you cannot get unstuck. New beliefs must be adopted in order to change the direction of your life. Remember, you must have a pretty clear idea of where you want to take your relationships before you start crafting your new belief systems.

Possible new challenging beliefs might be:

- I do not have to go to my parents' house every Sunday.
- I have a right to enjoy free time without feeling guilty about not being with my family.
- I have a right to limit contact with family that makes me feel uncomfortable.
- I can spend time with family I enjoy.
- I can leave a family gathering anytime I want.
- This is my life, and I am the boss over me.
- It's okay if my family does not "get" me.
- I absolutely do not need their validation.
- It's okay if I never get their validation.

4. Love Life

If you discover that you unconsciously believe love is supposed to be confusing, painful, aloof, frustrating, and/or that you do not believe love really exists at all, you will only create that reality in your adult life. What you perceive internally will manifest externally. If you want love in your life, you first must create love in your life. Love attracts more love. If you hate your Self, you must learn to love your Self and life before you can attract a love life.

Possible new challenging beliefs might be:

- Authentic, mature love does exist.
- I know love exists!
- I deserve respectful love.
- I am worthy of healthy adult love.
- I can attract a healthy mature adult.
- I want a peaceful relationship.
- I deserve a loving, empathic, romantic relationship.
- The more I learn to love me, the better my chances are of attracting love.

5. Physical Body

If you discover that you do not believe your body can feel any better than it does, or that you unconsciously presume you are powerless over how your body looks or feels, then you cannot possibly ever expect for your body to feel good. And since your body is the temple of your emotional soul, the better the condition of your body, the better your soul's ride through life. To feel balanced, we must tend to all areas of our life and not just one or two.

Possible new challenging beliefs might be:

- I can work out a few times a week.
- I can help my body feel and look better.
- I can walk every day.
- I can do some form of exercise every day.
- I can reduce my caloric intake.
- I can work out my heart.
- I can join a gym, or take a yoga class.
- I can commit to taking a multivitamin and multi-mineral tablet.
- I can get a checkup once a year.
- I will get that colonoscopy.
- I will make that dentist appointment.

6. Social Friendships

If you discover that this part of your life is unbalanced because perhaps you expect others to call you if they wish to enjoy your company, and you do not see yourself as the one who initiates the call, then you are leaving your social experiences in the hands of others. Without realizing it you are giving your personal power away by not choosing to decide how to spend your time and with whom.

If you discover you are spending time with people you do not care for, because unconsciously you believe it is hard to make friends, you will need to challenge that limiting belief in order to create a more balanced life.

Possible new challenging beliefs:

- It's easy to attract great friends when you know what kinds of friends you like.
- It's easy to spend time with people I really enjoy.

- I enjoy spending time with people who make me feel comfortable and happy.
- It's fun to do different things, even on my own.
- Taking risks oftentimes reaps great rewards.
- I can make friends easily.
- I want to make friends easily.
- I do not have to give up one friend for another friend.
- I can have lots of different social circles if I want to.
- I can walk away from any social circle when I want to.
- The right friendships enhance my life.
- I love being around fun people who enjoy the same things I do.

7. Money

If you discover that you have a fear-based relationship with money, it will be difficult for you to extract pleasure from the things money can bring you unless you focus on challenging that limiting belief.

If you discover that you unconsciously do not believe you are worthy of abundance, you will be caught in a never-ending tug of war between wanting and not having. Unconsciously you will have created a push-and-pull game surrounding money. Unless you confront your perceptions about money and work at reframing your relationship with money, you will be unable to attract the abundance you hear yourself wishing for and that you deserve.

Possible new challenging beliefs might be:

- Money actually does grow on trees.
- Money is not dirty.
- Money creates opportunity.
- Money is good.

- Money feeds people.
- Money clothes people.
- I can always make money.
- Money is my friend.
- I love money.
- It is okay to love money.
- Money is not the problem.
- Greed is a problem.
- Money is not filthy.
- Money is wonderful.
- Money is just energy.
- It's okay to love money.
- I am worthy of lots of money.
- I can share my money with others if I want to.
- I am deserving of nice things.
- Spending money responsibly on things that please me is a way I can take care of me.
- It's okay to spend money on things that I love if I spend responsibly.
- It's okay to buy myself something expensive once in a while—I am worth it!
- I can invest my money in me!
- Money is everywhere!
- If I can love my Self, I can love money and I can acquire great wealth.

8. Legacy

The inescapable universal reality of us all is death. Ultimately each of us will eventually take our last breath of glorious oxygen and depart from this wondrous planet. Facing our mortality helps us gain an appreciation for life that can be priceless. Consciously considering how those whose lives we have intersected with might speak of us when we are gone can help us crystalize our life's purpose. Doing so also assists our brain to utilize the pain-versus-pleasure wiring to our advantage, as coming nose to nose with our mortality allows us to more readily sift through meaningless clutter that may be taking up space inside our skulls.

As a young mother I experienced the untimely deaths of two women I loved. My first husband's sister died days after her twenty-ninth birthday. And my best friend Cathy died almost ten years later at the age of thirty-seven. Both of these women were mothers and had children who were three and eight.

Nothing can prepare you for the moment you are told that someone you love has died. When your loved one is particularly young and their death is untimely, accepting the reality of their passing can feel impossible. Losing someone at a tender age challenges the norms and standards we unknowingly abide by that act as mental bumpers as we go about our daily lives. Unconsciously we presume that our grandparents will die before our parents, and our parents will die before we do, and that our children will die long after we have departed. Although we rarely bring this framework to the forefront of our minds, many of us rest upon it regardless.

Being a part of the death experience for two young mothers crippled me in some ways, and freed me in others. Observing these women's babies observe them in coffins made death very real. Holding my sister-in-law's three-year-old daughter in my arms as she gathered flowers from the arrangements sent to the funeral home so we could make a bouquet for her mommy to take to the angels paralyzed me on the inside, although I appeared as strong as a skyscraper on the outside. I felt like I had to be the support this child needed, as her grandparents, father, and uncles were beyond consolable or available to her.

Fewer than ten years later, I found myself dazed by the reality that yet again I was holding another three-year-old child beside their mother's lifeless body. Not yet fully recovered from losing my sister-in-law or completely healed from my divorce, losing Cathy pushed the grief meter to tilt.

With a stiff upper lip, I remember struggling to force my mind to reach for a thought that would somehow soothe my mind and spirit. I remember the tug of war and the battle that raged within my heart and mind between despair and determination. Like so many times before, my children were my biggest motivation. For them I had to find a way to accept my dear friend Cathy's death, regardless of how distraught I felt about it. My divorce from my children's father taught me much about accepting what one cannot change. I did my best to apply the lesson to this latest gut-wrenching actuality, as I was now face-to-face with the fact that there was no way I could ever grant my children the guarantee that their mother would not die when she was a wrinkly, senile old lady.

It was the concept of harnessing this experience and turning it into a possible life lesson for my children that allowed me to claw my way out of the quicksand grief can be. Along with learning lessons about accepting things I could not change was the profound understanding that those *things* included emotions. I decided that I would not shield my children from my tears of sadness, and that while expressing my emotions about Cathy's death, I would at the same time speak to my children about accepting that I had no control over this new reality. I hoped that by modeling raw emotions for my children, while at the same time addressing the concept of non-control through acceptance and surrender, perhaps maybe, just maybe, some good might have come from losing my friend.

Losing these two young moms taught me many surprising lessons. One lesson in particular has helped shaped my recovery process in a way I could have never imagined. So ordinarily consumed by everyday minutia, like dentist appointments, missed child support payments, games my ex-husband would play, rumors about my divorce, or the kids' dirty socks being stuck in the sofa, *again*, standing amongst the sea of mourners at Cathy's wake made me realize how insignificant most of what I was experiencing day to day really is.

So often Cathy and I had had conversations about things that now seemed so frivolous. We bitched, like most young mothers do, about laundry, the kids fighting, our husbands, the rude clerk at the bank, the rain, the humidity, and things like the new nail polish remover that did not hold up to its advertisement claims. Standing there, peering out amongst the waves of tears and grief-stricken faces, I would have given anything to have her back so we could have had a second chance at living a moment that was focused on love of something…anything.

Now that Cathy was gone, all we could talk about was the way she made us feel when we were around her. From the women Cathy had met at her new craft class, to the people she had danced with in her German dance group since she was a small child, to those of us in her tight, close circle of friends, the only thing we were interested in talking about was how this vivacious, larger-than-life woman was able to make us feel seen, validated, and heard regardless of how mundane our conversation.

This ability to connect with people and make them feel seen was and is Cathy's legacy. If you were Cathy's friend, you knew it. If Cathy said she loved you, you could rest assured that if you needed her at 3 a.m., she'd slap on her frosted lip-gloss and find you. In the sea of mourners, there was not one person who did not express similar sentiments for my friend. It was Cathy's legacy that I clung to as I glided through that overly fragrant room, slid my warm hands over her cold ones, ran my fingers through her children's hair, gently kissed mourners hello and Cathy good-bye.

Losing these two young mommies in many ways got the splinters out of my ass. Death would come for me just as it had come for them, eventually. One day it would be *me* my loved ones were discussing. The bumpers off now, I began to assimilate, however apprehensively, the notion that in life nothing was guaranteed. These two deaths taught me the meaning of impermanence, even in the most sacred things. There is no mother, child, father, church, or hillside that is safe. All that is, is subject to the laws of nature. The force behind all that is unfolds according to laws set in motion ions ago. One day all that we know will be no more. We humans are powerless to the schedule a thing follows toward its final transition.

There is nothing one should attach to, as all that is, is impermanent. This is the lesson I wished to share with my children. I prayed they would be so full of Self-love and Self-reliance that in spite of how much they may have loved me, if I died unexpectedly, my dear children would be able to move on, thrive, and even excel in spite of losing their biggest cheerleader. I wanted to teach them to love completely, and to give of themselves fully, like Cathy did, but to do so unattached to any outcomes or payoffs. I wanted them to live as if they were dying, and aware that each moment was a gift. I knew that if I could pass these lessons on to my children, and if they would adopt them, Cathy's death would not have been in vain.

If you have lived your life loosely aware of your own mortality, and you have not given a substantial amount of consideration to how you would like to be remembered when you die, you may unconsciously perceive your time on this planet as infinite. Avoiding thinking about your mortality may be adding to your procrastination and desire to manifest true health. So many of us say, "Oh, it will get better one day," as one year rolls into the next. Confronting your mortality head-on will help you better be able to develop a game plan moving forward as well as create a specific timeline you can adopt to plot your recovery progress. Your time here is limited, Dear One. None of us escape on our feet.

Time is the only thing you can give away and never get back.

Possible new challenging beliefs might be:

- Life is not a dress rehearsal.
- My life is going to end.
- I can make changes now.
- I only have a limited amount of time to manifest my happiness.
- I honor my personal time.
- I can better manage my time.
- I can make better use of my time.
- I can work on leaving behind a legacy I can be proud of.
- I want to be known as someone who was not afraid to try.
- I want to be known as someone who loved deeply.
- I want others to remember me as full of laughter.
- I want others to remember me as being victorious over adversity.
- I have no time to waste trying to convince people I am worthy to be loved.
- I am worthy to be loved.
- I am love.
- I am no longer willing to wait to be happy.

- I can create my own happiness.
- I can create my happiness right here and right now.
- I can harness the power of my awareness.
- I can shift my focus.
- I can focus upon lovely things no matter what is going on around me.
- I know that if I maintain my mental focus, I can shift my reality.
- I am no longer willing to wait to feel free.

AIMS ACHIEVED BY INCORPORATING THIS REWIRING EXERCISE

All that we believe is the result of consistency and repetition in our thought processes. Many of us are unaware that our internal dialogue is the result of childhood brainwashing. However our parents perceived money, jobs, security, love, romance, the rich, the poor, society, government, different religions, god, different races, and the like is generally how we unconsciously perceive these things as well. The way our parents perceived us, or the way we presumed our parents perceived us, also impacts how we see Self today. Until we challenge these beliefs and create new beliefs in place of the old ones, we remain stuck in the past and behave more like zombies than we do divine human beings with the ability to resurrect our own image of Self—with the ability to create unique desired realities versus unwanted realities.

It is possible to die to the old and be born again in a new light body, but not until you first confront the shadows within. These shadows represent your false self. They are a manifestation of the ego mind and were created through the perceptions and beliefs of other's deluded egos. To live your new life in your new body, you must first clear your mind of any programming that is false and of the world. Your false self is an illusion, *but* your mind does not know that. Healing will require you to literally create your new Self. Just as Rome was not built in a day, nor is the ability to integrate the mind with a new perception of its true divine nature. You may have been told your entire life in big ways and in small ways that *you are not enough*. For many years you may have been telling yourself the same story. To heal, you will need to address the beliefs that are at the root of your unnecessary dissatisfaction with life.

Incorporating this strategy into your life will help you learn how to seek pleasure in ways you never imagined. No longer addicted to pain, you will begin to slowly become less hypervigilant and more pleasure seeking. Without consciously realizing it, you will be seeking the light within; the light that you are; the light of your world.

11. Struggle With Intimacy

Intimacy requires us to be vulnerable. It also requires us to be honest, open, trusting, and emotionally available. But when you are a being who has been brainwashed to believe you are unworthy and/or not enough, the emotions that naturally accompany beliefs like these are crippling. They inhibit our ability to develop any flow of the vibration that is love. Guilt, shame, fear, unworthiness, anger, and intimidation are just a few of the emotions that partner corrupt beliefs and create the angst that is the byproduct of the illusionary false Self. This angst is like a clamp that prevents us from being able to receive and give love in healthy, authentic exchanges.

Throughout our lifetimes, those of us who have been abused have a difficult time being intimate with others in the purest of ways. Although we crave love, affection, attention, and physical closeness, we fear it as well. We may entice future love interests or friends with a cleaned-up version of our false Self, but beneath the surface we feel like phonies— as if we are lying to those we spend our time with. This is a sense only we can acknowledge, and it eats at us slowly, which only compounds our internal guilt and shame.

Our inability to be vulnerable is the result of being taught to believe something about Self that was simply not true. We were never not enough, and at our core we are divine ~ period! However, until we learn to stop pinching ourselves off from our true divine nature, we will stay stuck in mental and emotional loops created by our childhood programming. It is essential we step into our roles as victors and out of our roles as victims if we are to master the ability to be intimate with others in a healthy way.

Until we learn to free our innocent minds from the negative attitudes and opinions that prevented us from connecting to our personal divinity, it will be difficult for us to *release* the "need" to protect others from seeing our false Self. When we learn to reframe our perceptions of our younger Self, eventually forgiveness and acceptance of all that has been allows us to better perceive ourselves as victors rather than victims. Then and only then can we ever learn to love without being attached to someone else's validation, or some fantasized future outcome.

Learning to love from the heart is learning to love in the Now, unattached to the past or to the future. Loving from the heart implies you have learned to love Self first, and that you are now sending love from a place that is free of Self-judgment, that is unconcerned with other's judgment of you as well. You have found your center and you are now grounded in your personal truth. You have learned to accept and shed any lower version of Self, and have now shifted into a higher state of consciousness that has permitted you to accept your personal crown of glory. You are an angelic being and always were, Dear One. You are now beginning to believe in your innocence and divinity.

Beating Ourselves Up For Things That Were Not Our Fault

So often we berate ourselves without even consciously knowing it. When we forgive ourselves, as well as the negative programs rolling around in our heads, instead of berating ourselves, we step out of the role of victim. The victim mentality keeps us stuck. This mentality is rooted in powerlessness and lack. This type of energy acts like clothes-pins that pinch our beings off from the stream of abundance, which is actually a stream of pure, positive love. Whenever we label ourselves as stupid, fat, ugly, dumb, unworthy, and/or undeserving, we literally pinch ourselves off from the stream of well-being.

Within each of us is the ability to choose (free will) to STOP pinching ourselves off from the energy of love. When we stop pinching ourselves off from love, we learn to allow love to flow into our hearts and minds. When we learn to accept that we are love, we no longer see ourselves as unworthy or undeserving of love from others. When we no longer accept the labels others put on us, we have successfully healed any false perceptions of Self, and we know beyond a shadow of a doubt we have nothing to be ashamed of. When our shame is healed, we no longer fear being intimate and vulnerable with others. We have learned to see ourselves as divine spiritual beings, caught up in mortal flesh suits, who are trying to interface with a computerized brain that has been downloaded with dysfunctional viruses. When we are able to accept that our human condition is the result of false data being downloaded into our computer hardware, and that at our core we are divine, it helps us release any unnecessary guilt that has hindered our spiritual growth. When we successfully integrate our divine truth with our for-givable human truth, we become born again in our new mind, and begin to live our lives through our light bodies. Born again, we finally understand what it means to be the creator of our own realities. Each of us is god. Our DNA is coded with the ability to harness personal powers beyond human comprehension. Within each human being lies the ability to either create or destroy one's Self, and/or one's world as one knows it. Just as god creates or can destroy, man possesses the same divine ability. The tool of creation is love. The tool that destroys is simply a lack of love.

Staying In The Flow

Flow is all about going with love energy rather than against it. There is but one law that governs all that is, and that is the law of cause and effect. If you were taught you were unworthy, then you now believe yourself unworthy. If you believe yourself unworthy, you will carry guilt and shame. If you carry guilt and shame, you will fear letting people in because you will live in fear of them seeing your shame. You will fear being judged and abandoned. If you live in fear of being seen, you will hide. If you hide, you live an untruth. If you live an untruth, you will feel like a phony. If you feel like a phony, and yet expect your partner to be honest, you will believe your partner untrustworthy, as you will only be able to see in them what you see in Self. If you have been abandoned by those you loved, then you will fear getting too close to those you love today, because you will fear them hurting you by possibly abandoning you again. The lesser of two evils might be to simply shut oneself off from others.

The brain's attempt to keep us safe from pain might be to simply cause us to stay small and retreat behind the walls of ego. There, behind the invisible walls, our brain believes our tender souls are safe. The brain's defense mechanism needs a higher authority, a Higher Self, to input new data that allows for the computer's brain to reboot its perception of its Self so that the unnecessary walls can begin to crumble and the true Self can be set free.

Because life may have become about projecting your inner reality,
until you somehow learn to heal your inner false perceptions of
Self, you will sadly only recycle, recreate, and repeat the embedded
scenarios in your unconscious programming.
Although you crave love, you might continue to
sabotage your ability to sustain love.
Dear One—you are love!
There is nothing to fear…fear is the illusion.

When one lives their life through the false Self, one is out of the flow. To live through the false Self is to go against the basic and fundamental laws of the universe. This world is an abundant place, and there is nothing to fear. If you reveal your true human Self to someone and they reject you—it is not you they are rejecting. It is their inability to accept some human aspect of their own Self that they fear. You have just offered them an opportunity to heal, but due to their unwillingness to face their unnecessary inner shame, they may reject you instead, in an attempt to flee further from some facet of Self they do not know how to confront yet.

To be rejected by this person is actually a good thing. You are now free to attract someone who is more accepting, loving, authentic, good-natured, and kind, who also has the ability to be emotionally vulnerable in a relationship. When you choose to be in the flow of abundance, you eventually attract others who are as willing to be in the flow, as like beings travel on similar invisible wave paths.

If *you* reject others, then the key is to learn how to continually flow love to your own divine Self without the corrupt interruptions of programmed negative Self-talk.

You Are In Control Of The Flow

Mastering Self will require you to reframe your perception of Self. This exercise was designed to better help you step more fully into your role as the leader of your life. Being programmed to see Self as powerless has hindered your ability to use free will to your optimal advantage.

Yes, Dear Ones, we have the ability to control the flow of abundance in our lives.

Let's play with that concept and learn to apply what we have learned into other areas of our adult lives.

Thus far you have learned that desire, intention, discipline, detachment, seeking the higher mind, silencing the inner judge, acceptance, feeling, action, commitment, surrender, and refusing to think like a victim are some of the main keys to healing the illusions that have led to our inability to move beyond our childhood programs. In this strategy step, we learn to more fully comprehend what it feels like to clamp ourselves off from the flow of Self-love and how to consciously choose to release the clamp and go with the stream of abundance.

Strategy Step
Releasing The Clamp Exercise

Goal:

The goal of this strategy step is to learn to actually connect to the feeling of release to allow a deeper sense of connection to the true Self. Owning our free will helps us learn how to take the clothespins off, which allows us to flow more freely with the stream of abundance and stay connected to our divine god Self. Your free will is your most underused tool in your spiritual shed.

In this strategy step we are going to help your body and mind better acquaint themselves with the feeling of release so you can identify and apply that feeling to your healing work. It will also help you better acquaint yourself with the concept of free will and choice. Your free will is a godlike ability. On our journey, we have the choice to invoke it or not. I believe free will is what Shakespeare was referring to when he said, "To be or not to be. That is the question."

Essentially, this exercise will help you step more fully into your personal leadership position. You are the CEO of your life, and you get to make all executive decisions, including what memos stay and what memos get tossed. You are the creator of all that is, and this exercise will help you more fully integrate the feeling of stepping into the divine power that is made possible through free will.

You will need:

- Clothespins (one or two should do)
- Journal
- Pen
- Sacred space
- A trip to a park
- A moment with the moon
- A moment with the sun
- A moment with a beach or a beautiful view
- A moment with the sky

Part One:

In your journal please make a list of some of the negative words you use when referring to your Self. What does your negative self-talk sound like?

We all have unique words we use to identify ourselves when we are alone and we make a mistake. My favorite is "Lisa, you stupid ass! What the hell is wrong with you?"

When I clearly learned to identify all the ways in which I was emotionally and verbally abusing my own Self, it became obvious I had become my own worst enemy. Learning to forgive the program in me to Self-abuse helped me transform my life in innumerable ways.

Part Two:

In this part of the exercise we are going to be toying with the feeling of relief—relief we get to control. When you have completed your list, take out a clothespin and clamp it onto the fleshy part of your left hand between your pointer finger and your thumb. The clothespin should be uncomfortable, but not terribly painful. Now read your negative Self-talk aloud.

Once you complete reading your list aloud, release the clothespin and sit in the feeling of relief. For a moment, sense the release and the relief in your palm. Connect to the feeling emotionally.

Repeat this exercise at least five times.

Part Three:

Integrating Nature

For this part of the exercise, we are going to be helping you become more in touch with nature. There is a tremendous amount of knowledge we can learn by tapping into nature. By *tapping into*, I mean *tuning into* instead of *pinching ourselves off from*.

Although the sky is a moving canvas and birds are flying acrobats, those of us who are stuck in endless mental loops oftentimes stay cut off from the most divine aspects of the universe we all share. The universe is abundant and it is only our perception, which has been tainted by those we trusted when we were young, that needs to be amended. The world was *never not abundant* and we were *never not divine*.

- When possible plan a trip to a local park that is full of trees, hills, flowers, or perhaps wildlife.
- Take your clothespins with you.
- Find some time to sit by yourself.
- Take a moment to look around you.
- Clear your mind as best you can.
- Place a clothespin on the fleshy part of your palm between your pointer finger and thumb.
- Tap into the feeling of being cut off and having your attention diverted from the beauty around you.
- Now release the clamp.
- Sit with the feeling of release and as much as possible try to absorb the beauty around you.
- After a few moments, clamp your palm again and once more sense how you can be pulled out of alignment with the beauty around you by pinching your hand.
- Release the clothespin and again tap back into the beauty around you.

Write down any emotions and/or insights this exercise has offered you in your journal.

Ask yourself these questions:

- What new sounds did I hear today when I released the

clothespin from my palm?

- What beauty did I find when I stopped pinching myself off from the abundance around me?
- What lovely things did I notice once I released the clothespin from my palm?
- What feelings did I feel when I noticed something new?
- What colors did I see when I stopped focusing on the feeling of being pinched off from the stream of abundance?
- How can I connect to the feeling of abundance—the raw state of nature—more often?

Please use this exercise often. I have used it while sitting on the back deck of my home, staring up at the moon and the stars. I have used this exercise at the beach, in a crowded city, and at a shopping mall. I have used this technique while speaking with one of my children. Without them knowing, I pinched my palm tightly and then released it to help me stay more focused on what they were saying. When I catch myself falling into unconsciousness and sense my mind running rampantly, I have trained myself to pinch the fleshy part of my palm with the opposite hand to help me remember that the present is a *present*.

Aims Achieved By Incorporating T he Releasing-The-Clamp Exercise

By incorporating this strategy into your recovery process, you will have successfully learned how to more easily control the flow of your Self-talk. So many of us do not realize we spend most of our time in the conscious mind, obsessing about the feelings that are being generated from the sub-conscious mind, and not in the higher, more aware, superconscious mind.

Einstein said, "We cannot correct a problem with the same level of intelligence that created the problem." Healing a dysfunctional belief that resides somewhere in our subconscious mind will require us to step into a higher state of consciousness. It will not be possible to heal while staying stuck in patterns created in the past, or while staying stuck in "what if" thinking about the future.

This exercise helps you stay out of the past as well as the future so you can harness more effectively your free will and begin creating effective change. You also learn to feel what it feels like to say no to your negative programming. You have the power to create your own reality. It is my prayer, that this exercise helps you more tangibly comprehend the powerful reality: You are the creator of your own reality, and you sculpt reality by way of your focus and thoughts.

12. Doubt Happiness Can Be A Reality

The "Why bother?" Attitude

Adult children from dysfunctional homes sadly learn to believe they cannot trust themselves, others or the world. Because their experiences with life have taught them to fear what others think about them, many ACoAs are unaware at just how full of doubt they really are. We abused children doubt the world can be a safe place, because we have no mental framework for safety. Because our caretakers either ignored our internal realities or criticized our emotions when we dared share them, we have not been psychologically validated. The experience of psychological invalidation has come with a heavy price.

The cost of psychological invalidation is Self-doubt. Children discover their sense of Self when others validate for them their internal experience. When little Bobby comes home and says his tummy hurts, his mother and father are supposed to validate that internal experience and help rectify it. When little Susie comes home upset because a bully made fun of her hair at school, her emotions are supposed to be validated by her parents. When one sibling harms another sibling, healthy parents are supposed to step in and stop the abuse, not instigate more abuse or ignore it.

The cost of psychological and emotional invisibility can last a lifetime. Not having our internal realities validated by the people we perceived as god has caused us to fill with Self-doubt. We doubt our right to be happy. We doubt we have a right to feel what we feel. We doubt what we think we heard other people say. When we attract abusive partners and they twist what we say, we doubt we have a right to stand up to them and defend ourselves or leave the relationship. We doubt we have the right to seek counseling. We doubt we have a right to complain or feel like we deserve more. We doubt we know how to follow our instincts or make choices that are good for us or our families. We doubt we can live on our own and support ourselves. We doubt every emotion, action, and thought we experience.

The Unimaginable Cost Of Self-Doubt

All beings struggle with some form of Self-doubt throughout their lifetimes at one point or another. An adult who has not been abused in childhood might doubt whether they can actually make a career out of being an artist, or they might doubt they can actually finish that marathon they have been training for. However, in spite of the occasional doubtful moments, Self-actualized adults tend to focus on the finish line and rarely get stuck midway like ACoAs tend to do.

Adult children from functional homes also tend to see the world through a much more pleasant eye than those of us from less than perfect homes. It is odd for us ACoAs to imagine that there are people who exist who actually do not doubt what they think, want, or desire. It seems impossible to believe that there are beings out there who connect with nature, live in the moment, and truly seek authentically pleasing experiences.

In my coaching practice I have had the pleasure of working with world-class athletes, doctors, and politicians, who, in spite of their professional accomplishments, suffer with looming Self-doubt on a consistent, gnawing level. Although they cognitively understand on some level that others might view them as one who has arrived, it is as if inside, below their skin, they fear being "found out." Regardless of how many awards hang on their walls or how many degrees they have accrued, viscerally there is this sense they cannot name that causes them to doubt they deserve to feel proud of what they have achieved. Self-doubt, like carbon dioxide, suffocates the joy right out of their inner being's ability to revel in any sense of personal satisfaction. Sadly, this is a state that most adult children can relate to that rarely gets addressed head-on.

Many of us do not realize we have deemed the world a frightening place. If our homes were littered with anxiety, insufficient boundaries, unfair rules, fear, complaining, and the like, we may presume that the world at large plays by the same rules we learned in our homes. If our mothers believed people were selfish, bad, no good, rotten, evil, and so on, then we may hold those same unconscious and unchallenged beliefs today. If our parents criticized or mocked us, we may distrust others and presume the world is out to get us. We may be projecting the need to defend ourselves onto others without even realizing it, and attracting the criticism we believe we are trying to avoid.

How We See The World Is How We See Self

Our eyes are literally the windows to our souls. What our soul sees through those windows is always a mirror to what our soul is witnessing on our inner movie screen.

If I am critical of the world and others, that is because I am living through the program labeled "criticism."

Why?

If I am critical of others, it is because there is data in my memory bank with instructions for how to criticize others.

Where would this data come from? The data stored in our memory banks with instructions on how to criticize others has been registered through our emotional experience of being criticized. The actual *feeling* of being wounded through the act of being criticized and thus rejected by Mother and/or Father imprints the brain with data that labels these types of events as painful. The problem is complex.

a) The data to criticize has been downloaded, so it is there we hold the instructions for how to criticize, because we have been programmed to do so. The lens we use to view the world has been cracked. Everything our internal as well as external eyes see is then criticized, including the Self, others, our children, the weather, religions, strangers, dogs, cats, and birds. Nothing in our experience is spared from the internal critic.

b) Because we have been criticized, we may believe the messages those critical messages created in us when we were innocent dear little ones. If dysfunctional beliefs were created about the Self, we now unknowingly project those ill feelings about Self onto innocent others, similar to the way we were criticized as children. We may also unconsciously operate to *hide* those ill things we think about Self from others, which then creates the sense within that we are phonies. This further complicates our guilt, shame, and Self-doubt.

c) Our brains have registered being criticized as a painful event, and so unconsciously we may criticize others first, and thus reject others before they have a chance to criticize and reject us instead. This forces us to stay stuck in loops of dysfunctional existences.

d) If our parents unknowingly taught us to fear the outside world, we may unconsciously perceive the world as unpredictable, and thus unconsciously operate to control it.

e) Seeing the world as non-abundant gives us the permission to be miserable and blame others for our unhappiness rather than taking responsibility for it.

f) Viewing the world as abundant forces us to get out of our comfort zone. The brain may then retreat, as living outside the comfort zone creates anxiety and thus pain.

g) Perceiving the world as a beautiful place means we will need to tell a new personal story. If the world is beautiful, then we will need to rewrite the story we tell others and ourselves.

h) For us to see the world as safe, we would have to learn to confront those old limiting beliefs, and learn to somehow trust the Self.

i) We do not see abundance because we have not been programmed to see abundance and good within ourselves.

Dear Ones, it is the Self we must seek first.
It is the Self we must learn to honor.
It is the Self we must learn to trust.
Your programming is an illusion.
The Self matters.

How you perceive your Self will determine how you perceive your world.
If you see lack in your Self, you will see lack in the world. When you learn

to believe that who you are on an intrinsic level is divine, you cannot help but see divinity everywhere your new eyes fall.
Decide you matter, and watch the universe come alive for you, as if it is the first day of your new life!

Shift In Perception

Up until now, this book has been designed to help you shift the way you see Self. At this point, however, we are going to be utilizing our ability to perceive in a whole new way. Our brains are miraculous, and although up until this point in our lives our brains may have been operating on autopilot, the reality is at any point we can learn to captain our own plane. The moment we wake up and begin to tap into our ability to be aware of the way we think, life is forever changed. Awareness is the threshold of new life. It is through awareness that we get to become reborn and resurrected of a new mind.

We are all multifaceted human beings, with data that has been programmed into our subconscious minds beyond our conscious control. However, this programming is NOT us. It is a thing that has been done to us. A human being at his/her core is a divine, perfect creature capable of anything he/she desires, as long as that being can separate his/her perception of Self from the injuries created by faulty childhood programming.

Strategy Step
Choosing To Change The Way I Look At Things

Goal:

The goal of this strategy step is to teach you how to deliberately flow your focus in the direction of those things that please you and bring you pleasure. By consciously choosing to flow your focus in the direction of lovely things, you are forcing your mind to rewire its old way of relating to the world. This major alteration in your focus allows you to begin shifting your mind from lack to abundance. It also allows you to begin seeking pleasure as opposed to simply staying stuck in endless loops of pain avoidance. Most abused adult children see the world with a *half-empty glass* kind of a perception. And that's fine as long as that abused child one day wakes up and realizes that it's not their fault they see the world in such a skewed manner. In fact, the only reason an abused adult child sees the world in a negative light is because they have been programmed to fear their inner and outer worlds, rather than to embrace them with an open mind.

Thanks to recent findings, we now know that the brain can absolutely rewire itself.

Neuroplasticity implies that the brain can reorganize itself. The brain can adapt and change according to one's experiences. If an abused adult child can learn to see him/her Self as innocent and a victim of abuse rather than deserving of abuse, then that being can successfully move beyond their limiting beliefs about Self and successfully relinquish doubt that happiness is a possibility. By shifting what one believes about the world, one can train the brain to begin associating life with pleasurable experiences as well as abundance.

One of the major issues we face as abused adult children is the way we interact with the outside world. Because we tend to be on the defense most of the time, we are rarely in the moment. So often stuck in our heads, we do not tap into the abundance that is about us, and tend to miss out on ample opportunities to feel connected to streams of well-being.

By forcing our brains to focus on things in our environment that please us, we are learning to rewire the way our brains are accustomed to dealing with the outside world. When seeking beauty becomes my focus, rather than worry about what someone else might be thinking of me, for example, I am able to effectively create change within me on a cellular level. I can be whatever I wish to be, but not until I am able to change the way I see my Self, and my world.

For this exercise you will need:

- Journal
- Pen
- Willingness
- Awareness
- 31 days

In your journal please make a list of the hours in a day, and draw a line next to each hour. You may block the hours you spend sleeping.

Every hour, beginning with the hour you wake up and ending with the hour you go to bed, you are going to force your mind to find something in your immediate environment that pleases you.

For instance:

- 6 a.m. I loved the way my pillow felt as I woke up this morning.
- 7 a.m. I love the way my coffee smells.
- 8 a.m. Our dog is so adorable.
- 9 a.m. I noticed that woman's hair color and I really liked it.
- 10 a.m. I really like my pen.
- 11 a.m. The carpet in this office is a nice shade of blue.
- 12 p.m. The sky is incredibly clear today. I like that.
- 1 p.m. This office plant is so beautiful.
- 2 p.m. I really liked the shoes Sonia wore today.
- 3 p.m. Those birds in that tree look so happy.
- 4 p.m. That was such a friendly cashier.

- 5 p.m. I love my car.
- 6 p.m. That dinner was fabulous.
- 7 p.m. This kiwi is really fresh.
- 8 p.m. That conversation with Cathy was so much fun.
- 9 p.m. I really enjoy how peaceful my house feels.
- 10 p.m. My bed feels amazing.

At the end of each day, you should have a long list of the things you noted in your environment that pleased you. For this exercise your goal will be to force your mind to notice things, people, smells, colors, conversations, and the like that please you.

At the end of thirty-one days, your mind will have developed a new habit. Your mind loves patterns. The goal is to teach your mind to begin seeking pleasurable experiences. For many of you, this will be a new way of relating to the world.

> "When you change the way you look at things,
> the things you look at change."
> —Wayne Dyer

AIMS ACHIEVED BY IMPLEMENTING THE PERCEPTION EXERCISE

By implementing this strategy into your daily routine, you will begin to understand the power of your own magnificent mind. Many of you are just beginning to become aware that your behaviors and thoughts are the result of programs that have been created by unconscious beliefs the authorities in your life taught you to believe through observation, consistency, and repetition.

This strategy was created upon the premise that through **deliberate** observation, consistency, and repetition, one can literally reprogram one's own mind.

As an adult, you now have the power to invoke your personal free will to choose how you wish to see Self and your world. When you learn to take control over your point of focus, you tap into the same energy that created the universe. As your perceptions about Self and your world begin to shift, so, too, will your manifestations. Feelings become things. What you feel will manifest, so working in the emotional realm is crucial to deliberately manifesting the desires of your heart.

Dear Ones, how you *feel* is everything. What you think is not as important as what you feel. If you think you wish to attract love, yet do not feel deserving of love, then you cannot attract that thing you think you desire. If you think you wish to be happy, but do not believe or feel happiness is attainable, you cannot attract the happiness you hear yourself thinking you want. If you think you wish to be healed, but do not feel you will ever be healed, you will be unsuccessful on your quest until your heart is in alignment with your mind.

Implement this strategy, and watch your world and your life come alive in a whole new way, Dear Ones. Each of us IS the creator of our own reality!

Namaste!

RECIPE FOR PERSONAL HAPPINESS

Whether we realize it or not, our lack of confidence is the result of a particular emotional recipe. What our parents put into our brain is what comes out of our brain. How we have been taught to perceive the Self is how we tend to perceive others.

If doctors know why a person has a specific disease, they can develop a particular protocol that increases his/her patient's chances of better health.

For instance, if I discovered that I had a significant cholesterol problem, and that my addiction to cheese was probably the root cause, my cholesterol recipe would look something like this:

Cheese + daily consumption = elevated blood cholesterol = increase risk of heart disease and stroke

Because only the law of cause and effect governs the universe, as an intelligent woman I would have to conclude that if I stopped eating cheese, my cholesterol levels would decrease.

My recipe for a new desired outcome might look like this:

0 cheese consumption daily = decrease blood cholesterol = decrease risk of heart disease and stroke

I could also conclude that if I stopped eating cheese, much of my anxiety and stress related to possible serious health issues would decrease, and thus my level of happiness would increase.

So What's The Recipe For Happiness?

In order to know what your personal recipe for happiness is, you first must know what your recipe for unhappiness looks like. If you were ignored as a child, then your recipe might look like this:

Being ignored as a child = learning to ignore Self = fear of others, shame, guilt, and overall unhappiness

In order to discover your recipe for happiness, you will have to call on the law of cause and effect to help you out. Quite simply, what goes in is what comes out. If you continue to operate your life by the same faulty principles the unaware authorities in your life programmed into you when you were an innocent child, you will stay stuck in endless loops of Self-defeating, destructive patterns.

As an adult, you must step into your adult role, invoke your right to free will, and take hold of your god-given ability to master your own reality. To help heal the above Self-defeating recipe for life, you will need to take an equal and opposite approach to that faulty programmed recipe. A new recipe might look like: **validating Self – fear of others, guilt, shame = happiness.**

Another recipe might look like: **validating Self = happiness.**

PERSONAL HABITS THAT INCREASE CHANCES OF BEING HAPPY

You are going to have to work at being happy if unhappy people have raised you. Sorry, Dear Ones, that is just the way it is.

Some of the qualities I learned to appreciate about teaching myself to be happy, in spite of being raised by unhappy people, are:

- Happy people rarely complain. They figure out what they want and every day find time to work toward that goal, sometimes in the wee hours of the morning. They don't adopt these kinds of habits to impress others. They adopt these habits as a way to honor their own path, and to seek pleasing the Self.
- Happy people don't require other people's validation. They honor the guidance from within, set a course, and tend to that course in their own time.
- Happy people don't criticize others. In fact, happy people praise others and offer compliments freely from an authentic place, expecting nothing in return.
- Happy people tend to set personal goals.
- Happy people don't criticize themselves when they make a mistake.
- Happy people accept that they are works in progress.
- Happy people tend to appreciate nature, animals, the young, and the elderly.
- Happy people don't expect others to agree with them.

- Happy people don't attach themselves to outcomes. They do their best each and every day, and tend to revel in the personal satisfaction that comes from doing a job well.
- Happy people aren't afraid of making a mistake. In fact, happy people expect mistakes will be made, and see the mistake as an opportunity for personal improvement.
- Happy people follow their own moral compass.
- Happy people appreciate their own personal accomplishments. Even the small successes matter to a happy person.
- Happy people are less concerned with what others think of their accomplishments, and are more concerned with their personal victories along the way.
- Happy people don't gossip.
- Happy people tend to change the course of negative conversations to more positive subjects.
- Happy people embrace what is happening in the moment. If they are outside, they tend to be able to tap into nature quickly. They are able to leave their worries about work at the office, rather than carry that energy with them throughout the rest of their days or weeks.
- Happy people like to move their bodies. They enjoy sports, yoga, walking, hiking, dancing, and general exercise.
- Happy people tend to take pride in their personal hygiene.
- Happy people say what they mean and mean what they say. They will not babysit your children unless they really want to, which allows them to feel happy about being with your children if they choose to be, and with knowing they were able to help you out if they decide to.
- Happy people are honest with themselves and others.
- Happy people don't freak out when things don't go as planned. Instead they tend to take things in stride and tend to live by the idea that "this too shall pass."

- Happy people tend to compliment life, the earth, themselves, and others with doses of appreciation and gratitude.
- Happy people tend to live in a consistent state of gratitude.
- Happy people tend to see experiences as opportunities to grow, and that includes the painful ones.
- Happy people tend to refuse to let a negative outcome discourage them from playing in the game of life. A setback is just a bump on a long and winding road. It's nothing to pop a cork about.
- Happy people tend to accept that death is a natural part of this process called life. This facing of their own mortality only increases their thirst for more satisfying life experiences.
- Happy people tend to be interested in leaving the planet a better place than what it was when they arrived. Leaving some kind of a legacy behind is of importance to happy people.
- Happy people tend to feel connected to Self, others, the world, and even the universe.
- Happy people accept the cause-and-effect nature of the universe, and do not blame others for why they are not where they wish to be, yet.
- Happy people are Self-reliant.
- Happy people are solution-oriented and excuse-empty.
- Happy people seek pleasurable life experiences.
- Happy people accept the aging process with dignity and respect.
- Happy people tend to want to take care of their physical bodies.
- Happy people celebrate other people's personal victories, no matter how small.
- Happy people enjoy being loving.
- Happy people would rather be happy than in an unhappy, dissatisfying relationship.
- Happy people don't lie.
- Happy people are not ashamed of their family history. They

understand their history adds to the facets of the being they are, and offers opportunities to overcome as well as to learn how to be more loving and accepting of Self.

- Happy people avoid unhappy people.
- Happy people avoid drama, chaos, and turmoil.
- Happy people tend to enjoy music and harmony.
- Happy people don't perceive themselves in competition with others.
- Happy people are not in the habit of comparing themselves to others.
- Happy people trust their gut instincts, and don't waste their time trying to convince others to agree with them.
- Happy people can engage in conversations with others even if their personal opinions differ from the crowd's.
- Happy people tend to be those who have overcome difficult hardships in their younger years. It is as if the adversities of their youth have helped them weed out ideas and beliefs that do not serve them.

The world is a big place, full of approximately seven billion people, and every person has their own unique perception of this planet we all call home. Where you were born and to whom are just two of the many particulars that will affect your happiness equation.

If you lived in a third- world country that had limited access to clean water, it might make you happy to live near a freshwater stream. You might consider your life a huge success if you had trusted your gut instincts to march on that extra mile in the hot sun, although the elders of your community called you a fool for believing drinking water was near. In spite of what the majority may have thought, you tuned into your Self, tuned others out, and interfaced with your chakra system. By listening to your heart and attuning to the feeling of relief versus the feeling of constriction in your heart center, you stepped into the stream of abundance. The water your village was seeking existed. But because many did not believe that it did, to them it did not, until, of course, you took your beliefs on the road—and found your desires along the way.

IN CLOSING

It is possible to overcome your childhood programming. It is possible to uncover the secrets to the universe and to learn how to use the power of your own mind to create the types of life experiences you deserve. It is possible to love your Self, even if your family of origin was unloving. It is possible to learn how to honor your Self, even if no one ever honored you. It is possible to slash through the veils of illusions others created for you when you were an innocent being, and take ownership over the landscape of your own mind. It is possible because within you are the seeds of a god. It is time to awaken to your true nature, Dear One, and remember who you truly are.

Namaste…

CPSIA information can be obtained
at www.ICGtesting.com
Printed in the USA
BVHW03s0358230618
519772BV00002B/64/P

9 781478 772033